Llewellyn's

Witches' Datebook

2010

Featuring

Art by Jennifer Hewitson
Text by Elizabeth Barrette, Nancy V. Bennett,
Tabitha Bradley, Ellen Dugan,
Magenta Griffith, James Kambos, Mickie Mueller
Diana Rajchel, and Cerridwen Iris Shea

ISBN 978-0-7387-0693-1

2010

	JANUARY							FEBRUARY							MARCH							APRIL					
S	M	T	W	T	F	S	S	M	T	W	T	F	S	S	M	T	W	T	F	S	S	M	T	W	T	F	S
					1	2		1	2	3	4	5	6		1	2	3	4	5	6					1	2	3
3	4	5	6	7	8	9	7	8	9	10	11	12	13	7	8	9	10	11	12	13	4	5	6	7	8	9	10
10	11	12	13	14	15	16	14	15	16	17	18	19	20	14	15	16	17	18	19	20	11	12	13	14	15	16	17
17	18	19	20	21	22	23	21	22	23	24	25	26	27	21	22	23	24	25	26	27	18	19	20	21	22	23	24
24	25	26	27	28	29	30	28							28	29	30	31				25	26	27	28	29	30	
31																											

	MAY							JUNE							JULY							AUGUST					
S	M	T	W	T	F	S	S	M	T	W	T	F	S	S	M	T	W	T	F	S	S	M	T	W	T	F	S
						1			1	2	3	4	5					1	2	3	1	2	3	4	5	6	7
2	3	4	5	6	7	8	6	7	8	9	10	11	12	4	5	6	7	8	9	10	8	9	10	11	12	13	14
9	10	11	12	13	14	15	13	14	15	16	17	18	19	11	12	13	14	15	16	17	15	16	17	18	19	20	21
16	17	18	19	20	21	22	20	21	22	23	24	25	26	18	19	20	21	22	23	24	22	23	24	25	26	27	28
23	24	25	26	27	28	29	27	28	29	30				25	26	27	28	29	30	31	29	30	31				
30	31																										

	SEPTEMBER							OCTOBER							NOVEMBER							DECEMBER					
S	M	T	W	T	F	S	S	M	T	W	T	F	S	S	M	T	W	T	F	S	S	M	T	W	T	F	S
			1	2	3	4						1	2		1	2	3	4	5	6				1	2	3	4
5	6	7	8	9	10	11	3	4	5	6	7	8	9	7	8	9	10	11	12	13	5	6	7	8	9	10	11
12	13	14	15	16	17	18	10	11	12	13	14	15	16	14	15	16	17	18	19	20	12	13	14	15	16	17	18
19	20	21	22	23	24	25	17	18	19	20	21	22	23	21	22	23	24	25	26	27	19	20	21	22	23	24	25
26	27	28	29	30			24	25	26	27	28	29	30	28	29	30					26	27	28	29	30	31	
							31																				

2011

	JANUARY							FEBRUARY							MARCH							APRIL					
S	M	T	W	T	F	S	S	M	T	W	T	F	S	S	M	T	W	T	F	S	S	M	T	W	T	F	S
						1			1	2	3	4	5			1	2	3	4	5						1	2
2	3	4	5	6	7	8	6	7	8	9	10	11	12	6	7	8	9	10	11	12	3	4	5	6	7	8	9
9	10	11	12	13	14	15	13	14	15	16	17	18	19	13	14	15	16	17	18	19	10	11	12	13	14	15	16
16	17	18	19	20	21	22	20	21	22	23	24	25	26	20	21	22	23	24	25	26	17	18	19	20	21	22	23
23	24	25	26	27	28	29	27	28						27	28	29	30	31			24	25	26	27	28	29	30
30	31																										

	MAY							JUNE							JULY							AUGUST					
S	M	T	W	T	F	S	S	M	T	W	T	F	S	S	M	T	W	T	F	S	S	M	T	W	T	F	S
1	2	3	4	5	6	7				1	2	3	4						1	2		1	2	3	4	5	6
8	9	10	11	12	13	14	5	6	7	8	9	10	11	3	4	5	6	7	8	9	7	8	9	10	11	12	13
15	16	17	18	19	20	21	12	13	14	15	16	17	18	10	11	12	13	14	15	16	14	15	16	17	18	19	20
22	23	24	25	26	27	28	19	20	21	22	23	24	25	17	18	19	20	21	22	23	21	22	23	24	25	26	27
29	30	31					26	27	28	29	30			24	25	26	27	28	29	30	28	29	30	31			
														31													

	SEPTEMBER							OCTOBER							NOVEMBER							DECEMBER					
S	M	T	W	T	F	S	S	M	T	W	T	F	S	S	M	T	W	T	F	S	S	M	T	W	T	F	S
				1	2	3							1			1	2	3	4	5					1	2	3
4	5	6	7	8	9	10	2	3	4	5	6	7	8	6	7	8	9	10	11	12	4	5	6	7	8	9	10
11	12	13	14	15	16	17	9	10	11	12	13	14	15	13	14	15	16	17	18	19	11	12	13	14	15	16	17
18	19	20	21	22	23	24	16	17	18	19	20	21	22	20	21	22	23	24	25	26	18	19	20	21	22	23	24
25	26	27	28	29	30		23	24	25	26	27	28	29	27	28	29	30				25	26	27	28	29	30	31
							30	31																			

Llewellyn's Witches' Datebook 2010 © 2009 by Llewellyn Worldwide. 2143 Wooddale Dr., Dept. 978-0-7387-0693-1, Woodbury, MN 55125-2989. All rights reserved. No part of this publication may be reproduced in any form without the permission of the publisher except for quotations used in critical reviews. Llewellyn is a registered trademark of Llewellyn Worldwide, Ltd.

Editing/design by Ed Day

Cover illustration and interior art © 2009 by Jennifer Hewitson

Art on chapter openings © 2006 by Jennifer Hewitson

Cover design by Anne Marie Garrison

Art direction by Lynne Menturweck

Table of Contents

How to Use Llewellyn's Witches' Datebook

Welcome to Llewellyn's *Witches' Datebook 2010*! This datebook was designed especially for Witches, Pagans, and magical people. Use it to plan sabbat celebrations, magic, Full Moon rites, and even dentist and doctor appointments. At right is a symbol key to some of the features of this datebook.

MOON QUARTERS: The Moon's cycle is divided into four quarters, which are noted in the calendar pages along with their exact times. When the Moon changes quarter, both quarters are listed, as well as the time of the change. In addition, a symbol for the new quarter is placed where the numeral for the date usually appears.

MOON IN THE SIGNS: Approximately every two and a half days, the Moon moves from one zodiac sign to the next. The sign that the Moon is in at the beginning of the day (midnight Eastern Standard Time) is noted next to the quarter listing. If the Moon changes signs that day, there will be a notation saying "☽ enters" followed by the symbol for the sign it is entering.

MOON VOID-OF-COURSE: Just before the Moon enters a new sign, it will make one final aspect (angular relationship) to another planet. Between that last aspect and the entrance of the Moon into the next sign it is said to be void-of-course. Activities begun when the Moon is void-of-course rarely come to fruition, or they turn out very differently than planned.

PLANETARY MOVEMENT: When a planet or asteroid moves from one sign into another, this change (called an *ingress*) is noted on the calendar pages with the exact time. The Moon and Sun are considered planets in this case. The planets (except for the Sun and Moon) can also appear to move backward as seen from the Earth. This is called a *planetary retrograde*, and is noted on the calendar pages with the symbol ℞. When the planet begins to move forward, or direct, again, it is marked D, and the time is also noted.

PLANTING AND HARVESTING DAYS: The best days for planting and harvesting are noted on the calendar pages with a seedling icon (planting) and a basket icon (harvesting).

TIME ZONE CHANGES: The times and dates of all astrological phenomena in this datebook are based on Eastern time. If you live outside the Eastern time zone, you will need to make the following changes: Pacific Time subtract three hours; Mountain Time subtract two hours; Central Time subtract one hour; Alaska subtract four hours; and Hawaii subtract five hours. All data is adjusted for Daylight Saving Time.

Planets

☉	Sun	
☽	Moon	
☿	Mercury	
♀	Venus	
♂	Mars	
♃	Jupiter	
♄	Saturn	
♅	Uranus	

♆	Neptune
♇	Pluto
⚷	Chiron
⚳	Ceres
⚴	Pallas
⚵	Juno
⚶	Vesta

Signs

♈	Aries
♉	Taurus
♊	Gemini
♋	Cancer
♌	Leo
♍	Virgo
♎	Libra
♏	Scorpio

♐	Sagittarius
♑	Capricorn
♒	Aquarius
♓	Pisces

Motion

℞	Retrograde
D	Direct

1st Quarter/New Moon ☽   3rd Quarter/Full Moon ☺
2nd Quarter ☽   4th Quarter ☽

○ **Tuesday** ◄———— Day and date
1st ♎ ◄————————— Moon's quarter and sign
2nd Quarter 4:01 am ◄——— Moon quarter change   Planting day ➡ 🌱
☽ v/c 4:01 am ◄————— Moon void-of-course
☽ enters ♏ 9:30 am ◄——— Moon sign change/ingress
♄ ℞ 10:14 am ◄—————— Planetary retrograde   Harvesting day ➡ 🧺
Color: Gray ◄————— Color of the day

5

The Birdbath Faerie Garden
by Ellen Dugan

Here is a fun project for all garden Witches, whether they have plenty of outdoor garden space, or if they garden in pots and containers on a porch, patio, or deck. Have you ever considered building a faerie garden out of an old cement birdbath? It's a fun and easy project to do. This way you have an enchanting focal point in the garden and the Fae have a great little magickal space to call their own.

Many of us have an old-style birdbath in the yard that birds just seem to ignore, so why not turn it into a clever container garden full of magick and mystery? To begin, you will need a large, cement birdbath that's about four to six inches deep. Many styles of birdbaths are actually too deep for birds to safely use. If yours looks like a big, deep bowl on a stand, then you are all set.

If you want to buy a birdbath to turn into a faerie garden, I suggest you keep your eyes peeled. Shop the discount centers' garden sections and see what you can find. Also watch for sales at the end of the gardening season—late summer. That's when you will find the best bargains on gardening accessories like benches and cement birdbaths.

To begin the construction of your faerie garden, make sure the birdbath is clean and sturdy. Choose the location for the faerie garden and set the stand in place. Now carefully fit the bowl on top of the stand and make sure it is level and secure. Next, in the bottom of the bowl of the birdbath, pour in two inches of gravel for drainage.

(This is a vital step. If you do not add the gravel, your little garden will not drain properly.) Mound up the gravel just a bit higher in the center of the bowl.

Next, begin to build up potting soil on top of the gravel base and create a "hill." You want the hill to be at least eight to ten inches tall. Take your time and enjoy this part. Remember when you were a tyke and made a big sandcastle? That's what we are going for here. Take your time and build up the potting soil until you have a nice big mound of dirt. Make the hill smooth and even on all sides. Now pat the potting soil together firmly. (It will help if your potting soil is moist at this point.)

Once you have your little mound all patted firmly together, you will want to choose low growing and trailing plants to place into your faerie garden. Small violas (a.k.a. 'Johnny-jump-ups') do best in the spring and cool fall months. Remember that pansies and violas do not tolerate extreme summer heat. You may need to replace these as the season progresses. It's no big deal to pop them out and to put in a new flower. I do this all the time at home.

If you prefer to avoid the need to switch flowers during the summer, try the trailing blue lobelia. A hummingbird and butterfly favorite, you can't beat the true blue color of this flower in a container. I use this plant every year in my own birdbath/faerie garden. You can also try various shades of sweet-smelling alyssum or fragrant bacopa. Bacopa, with its fabulous scent and tiny white blossoms, is also a popular annual for tucking into hanging baskets and window boxes. Another beautiful choice is variegated and solid green ivy, which is sacred to the faeries. For faerie herbs, consider prostrate rosemary (a variety of rosemary that trails). Thyme works well in a birdbath because it stays low, or "creeps," and will trail beautifully over the sides. You could even use a variegated variety of thyme to add more punch to the arrangement. Also, certain types of low-growing sedums or 'Hens and Chicks' will work out well for hot, sunny spots. If you have shade for your faerie garden in a birdbath, then go with ivy, moss, diminutive varieties of ferns, or colorful impatiens. For shade-loving herbs, try ajuga or sweet woodruff.

Once you have considered your sunlight and shade requirements and have chosen the appropriate plants, take a large spoon and carefully dig holes into your mound of dirt and tuck the new plants in. Pat the potting soil down firmly around the plants as you place them. Arrange the various annuals and perennials close together so the faerie garden looks full right away. There is nothing sadder than a basket or container that is waiting to grow in. When the planting is complete, water the entire faerie garden by hand with a watering can. You'll need the water to absorb into the hill slowly, so it's better to water this container with a gentle trickle of water. (Do not spray the planted mound down with a garden hose.)

To finish off the faerie garden, add ceramic mushrooms on stakes—a very popular gardening accessory these days. Look for weatherproof miniature statues of faeries or gnomes and add one to the arrangement as well. You can also try to work in a few tiny ceramic faerie houses—just use your imagination and see what you can conjure up! Finally, to really kick off your faerie garden in a birdbath, add clusters of quartz or amethyst crystals. These are great for filling in any bare spots and give the miniature garden a sparkly, faery-tale look. Every child that has ever come to my gardens goes crazy over the crystal clusters. My neighbors' five-year-old daughter says that I have "diamonds" in my gardens.

Once you have the faerie garden decorated to your satisfaction and watered, the next step is to bless the faerie garden. You actually have many options when it comes down to astrological timing. If you choose to incorporate lunar planting, then you will plant your annuals in the waxing Moon to encourage luxurious growth. If you have planted perennials such as sedums, ivy, or hens and chicks, then you

would plant those in the waning Moon. Or you can live on the edge and plant up the faerie garden on a Full Moon day and take advantage of the extra punch of nature's magick. The day of a New Moon would be an auspicious time as well. That way you can take advantage of the new energy and the waxing magick of nature. It all depends on how you wish to work your own style of garden witchery.

A Faerie Garden Blessing

Place your hands over the planted birdbath faerie garden and gather the energies of earth, air, fire, and water from the natural world that is physically all around you. Visualize the blessings of the air and feel a gentle breeze wash over your skin. Listen for the delicate resonance of the faeries on the breeze and invite them into their new home. Experience the heat of the Sun as it beams down on you and encourage its light and warmth to tenderly encourage your plants to flourish. Touch the wet leaves of the plants that you have just set into their new home. See in your mind's eye that the element of water will help your plants to thrive. Finally, sense the element of earth all around you and acknowledge the sense of connectedness that you gain from working with the earth itself. Visualize that the new plants will spread out their roots in the birdbath and that they will grow strong and true. Now open your eyes and repeat the following charm three times.

> By the elements of earth, air, fire, and water,
> I invite the garden faeries into their new home.
> Created by this garden Witch with love and laughter,
> Here is an enchanted place all of your very own.
> By all the powers of the Moon, stars, and Sun.
> May you be at peace here, and bring harm to none.

May your faerie garden flourish and bring you many hours of witchery, joy, and magick. Blessed be!

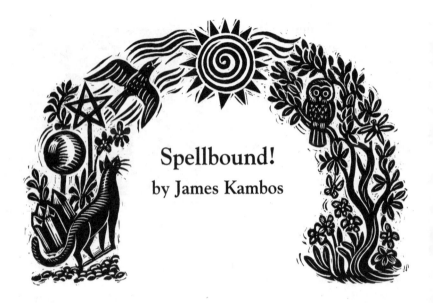

Spellbound!
by James Kambos

It happens to every Witch now and then. You ground and center. You speak words of power. You cast your spell and . . . nothing happens!

This is what I call being "spellbound." It's happened to me and it's no fun. So, what do you do when a spell doesn't seem to work? First of all, keep your cool and don't blame anyone, especially yourself.

Having written numerous articles on spellcasting, I firmly believe almost any spell that is conceived and performed with the proper intent will work eventually. Of course there are times when inexperienced practitioners may ask for something too far-fetched. For example, they may ask for a million dollars, when what they really need is a raise or the perfect opportunity to make some extra income.

There are times when a spell doesn't seem to work. It has been my experience, however, the moment a spell is spoken or written, it begins to take form in the Unseen Realm. Usually when a spell doesn't seem to manifest into what we want, it's because we've slowed it down somehow.

So, before you start kicking yourself because you think you've done something wrong, just take a breather. Relax, make a cup of tea, and let's take a look at why a spell can sometimes make a detour.

Purpose and Visualization

The objective behind casting a spell and seeing it physically manifesting itself in your mind's eye forms the base of most spells. Its purpose, combined with visualization, plants the seed for any spell.

There are two reasons why a spell could be sidetracked early on. One problem could be that you didn't state your objective clearly, or had too many thoughts at once.

Let's say you wanted a new home, but couldn't afford it. In this case, concentrate only on finding the home you want. By doing so, you'll focus on your real need, and chances are good the financial backing will fall into place. The Divine Spirit has a way of taking care of things like this.

The second problem concerns visualization. When you visualize your goal, you should see it completed. Using the new-home spell as an example, see yourself living in your new home, picking out the furnishings for it, etc.

If you aren't good at visualization, try this. Cut out a photo of your dream home from a decorating magazine. Look at the photo as you cast your spell; place it on your altar until your spell becomes a reality.

The keys to purpose and visualization are simple: Concentrate on one goal at a time, and "see" your goal completed.

The Power of the Spoken Word

After you've decided on your goal, you'll probably say a charm out loud or silently. This is where you put your goal into words. This is one of the most important parts of the spell and is known as words of power.

If not worded carefully, the spoken part of a spell can easily derail or misdirect any spell. Take care to word your spell precisely because you will get exactly what you wish for. Here are some pitfalls that you can avoid when writing and speaking your charm.

Remember, spells are affirmations. When you speak your words don't ask meekly if you can have something—declare it! It's OK to say something like, "The house of my dreams is coming into my life." Also, avoid phrases such as "I hope this happens." As long as it's a positive wish that won't harm anyone, you deserve it. If you feel you don't deserve something good, you'll be setting yourself up for failure.

One mistake some magical practitioners make is repeating the words of a spell too often. This is one of those times when less is more. If you repeat your spell too frequently, you're drawing it back to you, which will delay the spell in manifesting itself in your life.

There is no need to repeat your words or spell every day. My motto is "let it go and let it flow." If you must repeat your words of power or your spell, wait a month, or one lunar cycle.

If you should become impatient, instead of doing the spell over again, ask your favorite divining tool what's going on with your spell. I've found there's nothing wrong with consulting the tarot, runes, or pendulum regarding the status of a spell.

To sum up the three basic points to constructing successful words of power:

- The spoken words of a spell should be an affirmation.
- The words should be specific and positive.
- Perform the spell once and forget it.

Astrological Timing and Time Limits

Daily planetary influences and monthly lunar cycles can play a significant role in spells. Also, placing a strict time limit on when you want your spell to manifest itself in your life can have a negative effect on a spell. Let's look at both of these factors.

Not timing your spell with favorable daily and monthly astrological phases can slow down the speed at which a spell will do its work. This subject deserves an article of its own, but here are the main points.

Whether you realize it or not, we live with the rhythm of daily planetary influences and monthly lunar cycles. If you align your magic with the proper planetary/astrological timing according to your needs, you'll enhance the speed and power of your spells.

You don't need advanced astrological or Moon phase knowledge to harness the power of the planets. A good place to begin learning about the signs and Moon phases is in your hands. The daily planner in this datebook will give you all the basics you need.

When working with lunar phases follow this simple rule. To draw positive magic to you, cast your spell during a waxing Moon— New Moon up to the Full Moon. Just working with these fundamental principles will hasten your spells to fruition and increase your magical success.

If you're already working with astrological correspondences and your spells still aren't working, perhaps you've placed time limits on your spells, which can bring them to a screeching halt.

What I mean by time limits is when the magical practitioner states somewhere in the spell that the goal they wish for must occur on a certain day or by a specific time. Magic doesn't work this way. Time as we know it doesn't exist in the magical realm.

In occult theory, all time is now. What this means is that the past, present, and future are rushing about us all at once. So, if you cast a spell and say you need a $100 by Friday, it probably won't happen. This is a common mistake. To get around this, as you speak your charm say something like, "Bring me (your wish here) with perfect timing," or, "My wish is coming to me when I need it the most." Using this type of wording will release the spell's energy, and at the same time, you are affirming your trust in the Divine Spirit. As I said earlier, the Divine Spirit will take care of it.

The Divine Spirit Knows Best

There are times when you've cast your spell properly, but things may not turn out as planned. There'll also be times when your spellwork may go even better than you ever thought possible. That's because the Divine Spirit knows what we really need, and may even have something better in store for us. As an example, here's what happened to me.

Several years ago I rented a booth at a local art gallery to sell my artwork during a holiday art and craft show. Before the event I said my words of power to increase my sales.

I sat in my booth for two days; many people stopped by and I received lots of compliments. But, by the end of the show, I hadn't sold a painting. Disappointed, I packed up and went home.

Six months later, a man came up to me on the street and asked to see my paintings. He explained it was his father's birthday. I asked how he know about me, and he said he'd seen my art at the holiday craft show. And after his first purchase, he returned and eventually bought four more paintings!

That experience taught me a couple of lessons. First, it might take time, but a spell will manifest itself in your life. It also taught me that the Divine Spirit frequently brings us more than we could ever dream.

Believe in yourself. Believe in the power of your spells, and you will receive.

Computers and the Craft
by Magenta Griffith

Witches have taken to computers like ducks to water because the technology is incredibly useful. But are you applying your witchcraft to your computer?

For example, do you use magic to protect your computer? To physically protect your computer, use a guardian figure, like a small dragon statue or a small protective goddess or god image. Set this on top of your CPU or monitor. Invoke the spirit or deity and ask it to protect your computer and other equipment. Do not burn incense or sage around your computer, however. Smoke of any sort contains particles than can clog up moving parts, which can reduce air circulation and cause overheating. If you must use incense, do it when the computer is off. If you have a laptop with no place to put such a guardian, you can find a picture to put somewhere on your laptop or carry a tiny figure in your laptop case. You could even have your wallpaper display a protective image.

If you are keeping your Book of Shadows or other materials related to your Craft practices on your computer, you should consider either password protecting or encrypting those files. This is especially important if you share your computer, but useful even if you have your own. Computers may get stolen, and eventually you will upgrade and discard or recycle your old computer. Check the help files for your word processing program for details on how to password protect your special files. Many programs that compress files to save space also allow you to encrypt the files so that you must have a password to read them.

Your passwords can provide magical as well as mundane protection. Mix numbers and letters, and, if the application is case sensitive, mix upper and lower case. To avoid words found in an ordinary dictionary, go to an old grimoire or other book of magic that uses unusual words. Pick a few names that are associated with communication or protection. Associations with Mercury or Mars are good, but avoid evil or chaotic names. Change passwords on a regular basis, at least at every holiday, if not every New Moon. If you use numerology, the numbers may also be chosen according to your intent.

Of course you do regular backups. Wednesday, the day of Mercury, is connected to communication, so it's a good day if you do weekly backups. Do an extra set of backups a day or two before Mercury goes retrograde, when communication will be more difficult and more likely to get quirky.

Defragmenting the hard drive, often just called defragging, gets rid of the extra dead space, allowing you to store more information on your hard drive and enabling your computer to find that information more quickly and easily. Because this is a form of banishing, I would recommend that you defrag the hard drive during the waning Moon.

My favorite thing about computers is e-mail. I can e-mail my coven about an idea I've had for a ritual, or ask who left behind a baking dish, even though it's nearly midnight. I don't have to worry about who is awake, and I can tell everyone the same thing at the same time. (There are also file-sharing programs that can enable your group to share the writing and revising of rituals online.) One etiquette note: if you are sending e-mail to a larger group than your coven or other small group of friends, use "bcc," blind carbon copy, so the e-mail addresses of the recipients aren't displayed. It keeps people's e-mail address private, which is very important to some people in the Craft. It also keeps the display space smaller.

Since e-mail is all about communication, during Mercury retrograde be sure to reread everything before you send it to ensure it says exactly what you mean. Also, be sure to pause before responding to any e-mail sent. As you follow up, even if a message seems somewhat alarming, be prepared to cut other people more slack about what they intended to say during this time because Mercury retrograde affects everyone, whether they know about astrology or not.

If you are online, you have to decide how much you want other people to know about you and your practices. Would you prefer that people like your employer or your landlord not know you are a Witch? Pick a pseudonym that resembles neither your legal name nor your Craft name. Get a separate e-mail account from a free service such as Gmail or Yahoo! Mail. Give as little information as you can, such as giving only the city you live in, or the general area. Since many online sites want your name and e-mail, it's not a bad idea to come up with a name and e-mail address you use only for surfing, to keep your main e-mail address from attracting so much spam as to make it unusable.

Other things you can do to protect yourself online, besides the usual mundane warnings, include spells to keep away viruses and other malware, and against spam. Make a talisman in the shape of your cursor icon, an arrow, for example. Color it bright red, or make it out of red paper. In black letters, write the word "avert." Chant "avert virus, avert spam, avert worms, avert harm," several times, ending with "Avert!" shouted as loudly as you can. Fasten this to the upper right corner of your monitor, with the arrow pointing toward the center of the screen.

If you want to attract people to your Web site, come up with a short phrase that sums up your desires: "Buy my magical herbs," or "Join my

group." Reduce the phrase to one "word" made up of the nonduplicate letters, for example, "readmyblog." Place those letters in the html or other code for the page in such a way that it doesn't display. Another way is to come up with a sigil of attraction, and place it in the background of your Web page nearly—but not quite the same—color as the background. As an added bonus, doing this will also enable you to find out if someone is copying your Web pages and using them without your name.

There are many Web sites for Witches, Pagans, and other magical folks. Like everything else on the Web, you have to use common sense when reading them. It helps to know what kind of site you are viewing. For example, the suffix of a site tells you what sort of organization runs the site. Dot com, ".com" means it's a commercial site. If it is supposed to be a commercial site, for example www.Llewellyn.com, that makes sense, because it's a business. Some large nonprofit organizations are also .com. A smaller nonprofit will be .org or .net, for example, http://paganpride.org, which is the organizing site for Pagan Pride nationwide. Here are a few sites I've found useful.

Witchvox

The Witch's Voice, www.witchvox.com, is the best networking site for Witches and Pagans on the Web. The content consists of news stories, articles, editorials, and book reviews, as well as an extensive database of networking contacts. This is the place to start when looking for resources, such as a coven to join or events to attend. The site has been up for more than ten years and has an amazing amount of information.

Pagan Pride

This event happens every fall all over the United States and Canada, in Europe, and at facilities for military personnel. Some local groups also sponsor fall equinox rituals and other events. These are free and open to the public. Most also sponsor charitable work such as food shelf drives. The main site, http://paganpride.org/, can help you find an event in your area.

Llewellyn Worldwide

Llewellyn's Web site, www.llewellyn.com, has an abundance of free information, as well as the opportunity to order the latest books, get a tarot reading, check the Moon's sign, and many other useful features.

The Covenant of the Goddess

Information about The Covenant of the Goddess, one of the largest and oldest Wiccan religious organizations, can be found at www.cog.org. The Covenant is an umbrella organization of cooperating autonomous Witchcraft covens, groups, and individual practitioners, and has the power to confer credentials on qualified clergy. It fosters

cooperation and mutual support among Witches and provides legal recognition as a religion.

Isaac Bonewits

The author of *Real Magic*, has an excellent, informative site with a lot links at www.neopagan.net His Advanced Bonewits Cult Danger Evaluation Frame (ABCDEF) is very useful in determining if a group is potentially harmful.

There are also a number of Pagan magazines available both in print and online. Check out www.pangaia.com for *Pangaia* and links to *NewWitch* and *SageWoman*.

Blogging is very popular in the Pagan community as elsewhere. If you're are practicing alone, it can give you a sense of community, sharing with other Witches whether they are nearby or across the country. It's a great way to share rituals with the rest of your coven; some covens keep a group blog, each member adding to it as they will. Blogs are a way to get feedback from a wide audience, as well as to keep many people up to date on your activities with one post. There are so many blogs and they change so quickly that there is no point in listing them here.

Blessed computing!

Portable Altars

by Tabitha Bradley

No matter what you call them, altars and shrines in some form or another are an integral part of most Wiccan, Pagan, and witchy work. My friends have had some beautiful home altars and shrines—many have more than one. I have set up various types of little "mini-altars" and shrines throughout my living areas, from houses to apartments to hotel rooms.

Of course, most of the time, we are faced with travel, packing, and storage limitations that make bringing regular-size tools, or in some cases, *any* tools at all, impossible. It's a good idea to have a plan for these situations in advance so you can just toss your previously packed "portable altar" in your bags and go.

When I travel, I've used some different kinds of travel altars and portable shrines. Over the years, I have developed several ways of bringing along at least some kind of devotional set, even if it was simply a tea light and small shallow dish for water.

When you're traveling, the best idea is to leave your valuable tools and other special items at home. Therefore, when you begin to plan your portable altar, you will need to decide if you want to include portable versions of the tools you feel are the most important to your personal spiritual practice. If you're not inclined to crafting your own portable tools, it's definitely worth it to look around online to see what other Pagan folks are offering for sale. Many Pagan suppliers and crafters are selling small-to-miniature versions of Craft tools through

auction sites such as eBay and online craft bazaars like Etsy.

There are many terrific things available now that are perfect sizes for a portable altar or shrine, in materials that make life much easier for the Witch on the go. It's not hard to find wooden, acrylic, bone, or even plastic athames; smaller versions of statues; small, attractive candle cups for tea lights, as well as tea lights packaged in plastic containers rather than aluminum. Craft stores have some amazing finds, such as unfinished wooden boxes, plaques, and various turned and carved shapes and figures that can inspire the creative imagination, as well as all the things needed to finish these any way you like. If you like role-playing and tabletop fantasy games, you're probably already familiar with these small metal models, which make wonderful miniature god and goddess figures for a portable altar set. You may paint them and they're made from nonlead pewter, plastic, or other materials that are safe for air travel. And they're tiny, which makes them easy to pack in something as small as a makeup bag or small tackle box.

It's always fun to browse the catalogs and craft sites to get ideas for items you might be able to make yourself. This is another advantage of easy Internet access. Patterns and instructions for a variety of do-it-yourself projects are available for free all over the Internet.

For the creatively adventurous, portable altars can take a nonstandard approach. Small charm and pendant versions of a variety of Wiccan tools can be found, which can be put to use in some very creative ways. An "altar charm bracelet" is one idea, a Wiccan prayer bead necklace or bracelet is another. By using a variety of charms and beads, you could put together a "circle-casting" bracelet, which, paired with a favorite circle-casting poem, can enable you to bring your sacred space anywhere you go. Using "altered art" techniques, you can create an altar in the most unusual places. Altering a book, a mint tin, or an unfinished pressboard or wooden box into a beautiful portable altar is both a fun and an intensely spiritual experience as you look for the types of images and objects you want to incorporate into your project.

Another different style of altar is the type contained within a blank book or notebook. Using illustrations of an altar, shrine, and tools, you create an altar that can be used by touching the objects and visualizing. I have heard of this kind of altar being used in military and other situations where having even one Wiccan tool may not be advisable. This altar, of course, requires a bit of mental concentration and discipline, like any form of meditation. It is a kind of prayer and can be explained as thus, if necessary.

An interesting twist on this kind of altar is the "virtual altar," which can be created on a computer. If you travel with your laptop, this is another option for situations where bringing altar tools and equipment isn't practical. With a little Web-design knowledge, you can make an altar to use in your Web browser, or if you have some skill with an art program, you might create an image to use. Of course, if you're one of those folks with programming abilities, I'm sure there are plenty of ideas you could develop into something that would be useful and engaging. You can already find some interactive altars and shrines to various deities online as well as some cleverly programmed metaphysical software CDs.

As you work on building your portable altars and shrines, do research on how other religions create and use portable devotional tools. You may find the perfect option for you, or you might be inspired to take an idea and develop and customize it to fit your practice. A number of different religions use prayer beads in various ways, including some Pagan paths. Learning about how these beads are used and the significance of the number, size, and composition of the beads as well as the meaning of other medals, pendants, and clasps on the string itself may give you some ideas on how you might include prayer beads in your own portable altar set. Items like prayer beads are perfect portable devotional and spiritual tools, which is why they are used in

religions such as Buddhism, where counting the number of repetitions of a mantra is said to be beneficial to the practitioner. The rosary in Catholicism helps a person in saying specific prayers in the correct order, for instance. Prayer beads are used in various Pagan practices as a memory aid and they can be incorporated into many different kinds of prayers, spells, and rituals.

I developed a portable shrine a few years ago that's small enough to be carried in a digital camera bag! It has come in very handy and I've enjoyed it quite a bit. So, if you need a quick shrine and have a spare camera bag laying about, here's the setup of the Camera Bag Shrine. I'm a Priestess of Bast, so my shrine was built with her in mind initially, but there's no reason you couldn't use this for any deity. (I've used this for Buddha as well.)

The Portable Camera Bag Shrine

All you really need is a nylon digital camera bag with adjustable strap. I use a camera bag designed for small to medium cameras. If you use a larger one you have room for more supplies or possibly a set of small altar tools, which could turn this into a portable altar. These are easy to find in most department stores for between $10 and $20.

• Three plain tea lights. These should be packed in a zipper bag to protect the other items in the case from possible wax damage if the tea lights should melt.

• One basic glass tea light holder. If you want to use a fancier one, that's fine, but it should be solid.

• One stoneware condiment dish. Mine is a Chinese condiment dish I found at an import store.

• A lighter, or a book or box of matches.

• Cone incense in zipper bag.

• Mini-ramekin or small porcelain dish. The idea here is that the dish should be heatproof. I use ramekins in larger sizes for loose incense on charcoal because the dish is designed to take heat and can be picked up and moved around if needed. Chain department stores will sell these in packages of two or four in the baking section. You may also find them in import and specialty shops.

• A small amount of the following: plain clay cat litter, plain sand, or salt in a zipper-close bag. For your incense burner, pour the chosen granular material into the ramekin dish, set the cone incense on top, and light. The clay cat litter is the best for this because it insulates very well and distributes the heat. You need to make sure that the litter is only clay—no other added scents or chemicals. Otherwise, sand or even salt will do in a pinch. You can also use this incense burner set to burn mini-stick incense, or the pressed Japanese and Chinese stick incenses. Many of these come with a tiny ceramic tile to place the stick in while it burns, which is also an excellent portable altar incense option.

(Instead of the cone incense, you can bring a zipper bag of mini-stick incense. This is the smaller version of the 'joss stick' Indian-style incense, which has become popular. You can get this kind in a multi-packs that sometimes come with its own little teak burner.)

• Mini stick burner. If you don't get one in a multipack of mini-sticks, you can usually find mini-burners in teak, soapstone, and even metal in import stores, chain department stores and craft stores. Or, you can always use the above ramekin suggestion with a dish of clay litter or sand.

• And last, but definitely not least, your god or goddess figure. It's much easier to find excellent small versions of deity statues now than it was even a few years ago. There are museum stores, importers, and specialty Pagan shops that are offering statues in various sizes, making it easier than ever to bring a beautiful representation of your god or goddess with you.

Even if you travel quite a bit, there's no reason you can't have an elegant and meaningful altar or shrine, no matter where you are. They can be as simple or as elaborate, as plain or as beautiful as you'd like and you can have fun putting one together, even if you don't consider yourself "crafty."

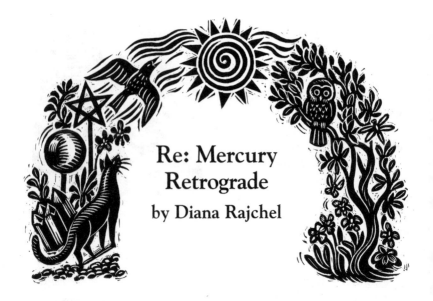

Re: Mercury Retrograde
by Diana Rajchel

Mercury retrograde, to most people, means duck and cover. Three times annually, Mercury appears to slide backward through that great natal chart in the sky, dragging along with it technology, travel plans, and the basic ability to interact. This is the time of flight delays, crashed computers, and intense, serious arguments about whether cavemen or astronauts would win in a fight. Mercury retrograde rivals the New Moon for statistically counted incidents of sheer craziness and if there is a New Moon during Mercury retrograde, watch out! Even those who don't follow astrology have asked in panicked bewilderment, "What the heck is going on lately?" when they experience the latest crash brought on by retrograde energy.

When Mercury retrograde happens, we could just hide. But twelve weeks a year is a long time to hibernate. Just ask a bear. Since most of us can't really afford that luxury, it's best to figure out what needs to be put on pause—and what can actually work while those lines of communication and commerce are stilled.

So, rather than hide, survive. You have plenty of warning about upcoming Mercury retrogrades in this datebook, which gives you a chance to prepare. The effects begin ten days prior to the cosmic event. Use your preparation time wisely—this is the time to back up all your data, export blogs and RSS feeds, and delete all those e-mails lingering in your trash bin. Communication will be more difficult, so having the information you're in charge of easily accessible will defuse a blowout.

Also, if you can, delay big decisions—put off closing on a house, do not take a trip in a country where you don't speak the language well, and delay the wedding date. I would even suggest you put off selling a used car, lest you unexpectedly be hit with a lemon law.

So, with that list of "don'ts" covered, I bring you to the list of "dos." Mercury retrograde is an auspicious for certain tasks. Just keep in mind the prefix "re." It is a good time to reread, review, reconsider, rewrite, and redo some projects. Mercury retrograde is also a time that lost things return to you—those papers you misplaced a month prior will likely turn up. So will your spare keys. You can also use this time for deep internal psychic work that demands repeated practice and reflection.

Since you have three weeks of Mercury retrograde to look forward to, schedule points of time during the three weeks for quiet self-examination and cleansing. Look deeply at yourself, but do not look too deeply at others—Mercury retrograde is a time to reveal to the Self and the Divine, but revelations from others is at their discretion, not yours. You may want to try a three-week program just for Mercury retrograde: during week one, reexamine your living situation. This is an excellent time to clean your home of excess junk and take it to a thrift store or have a yard sale. Yes, commercial transactions are iffy, but if you do the yard sale, keep in mind it's not about the money—it's about alleviating the burden of your own excess. Take stock of what else may have turned up in your evacuations: did you find those library books you meant to return two months ago? Did you find an old bill underneath a table? Did you find some project you abandoned because of time constraints? Is your recreational e-mail account or your Twitter bulging with old messages?

Return those library books. Pay the bill you missed. Resume that project, and do what you can to finish it within the three-week period. While you may encounter some challenges—an unusual traffic jam on the way to the library, the newspaper leaving a typo in your address when you advertise your garage sale—you will still be opening yourself to the internal journey that Mercury retrograde is for. Your methodical examination of goods to keep and dispose of will turn up things you have overlooked, forgotten, or misplaced. Mercury

retrograde slows down the pace of life and gives us a chance to recapture otherwise missed opportunities, and in a small way, gives us a chance to recapture ourselves.

Other complications beyond household concerns are bound to crop up, usually during the second week. For instance, every Mercury retrograde, I hear from someone I lost touch with. Sometimes I don't want to get back in touch with that person, sometimes I do, but it always leads to the final conclusion of some old business between us. You can take advantage of this energy to clear out your own unfinished business. Use your second week of Mercury retrograde to get in touch with people you've lost contact with but want to hear from. Clean out your e-mail inboxes. Check the blogs and forums you've let languish. Sift through physical and computer files to determine if you really need to keep the stuff clogging up your virtual space. Write letters. Update your virus programs, take your car in for a tune-up, and since you're cleaning your files, review the warranties on all your old appliances. Even shop around to make sure you're getting the best insurance rates. Take the time to reread contracts you've signed. While Mercury retrograde can befoul communication, it can enhance our ability to receive information and to catch details ordinarily missed in life's daily rush.

Since the second week of Mercury retrograde is the deepest week in, I recommend grabbing any solo time you can get. It's a great time for psychic exercise: with communication slowed, you can plunge into sixth-sense work. If you want to sharpen your understanding of tarot, start your journal by going through one card at a time and writing as much as you can on the meaning you see in the imagery. Practice new meditation and trance techniques. See what you can do with a pendulum. This is an excellent time also to reinforce protective wards on your home and to cast spells promoting harmony and health. Journal, meditate, and think as much as possible throughout the retrograde. While it may be difficult to share the product of your work at this time, you will have much to offer at the end of the three weeks in the form of refined practice.

Unless you live in a very isolated area, it won't be possible to spend all your retrograde time alone. In order to smooth those unavoidable interactions, use a "pick your battles" approach. This is not a time to deliver criticisms that aren't crucial. Don't tell someone he or she has been passed over for a promotion, and if you're considering ending a relationship, or are trying to start one: hold off. Information you need to smooth everyone's path will be forthcoming at the end of this time period. Some of that information could well change the way you feel about the people around you. If you must schmooze, talk about television and movies, gardening and food—relatively non-controversial stuff. Among magical types, this may be very difficult: sex, politics, and religion are often our only topics of discussion, with the occasional recipe or garden tip thrown in. Still, it's possible to keep it pleasant with a bit of polite concentration.

Week three is the final closeout of Mercury retrograde and time for you to complete your retrograde projects so you can reengage with the world. I think of this as damage-control week. This is the time to fix all that ran amok as a direct result of retrograde; it is also the time to schedule and plan what happens in following weeks: set up appointments to meet with people about new projects, organize notes and other materials and put finishing touches on work coming due.

Ideally this approach to Mercury retrograde will leave you unscathed and in touch with the benefits of retrograde energy. It is my hope that after all that your computer works, your car runs, you know where your passport is, and you still have a home. Sometimes change is inevitable, but hopefully, with careful management, you'll come out of the three-week period feeling internally cleansed and having embraced all resulting changes as beneficial.

Mercury retrograde can be our ally, but it requires setting aside the breakneck pace at which we've set our lives. Those time-off periods that Mercury engages in? Those are signals for us to follow that energy in a little time off, too. It's the time to do all the things we mark for "later." Mercury retrograde is the time of 'round to it—all those things you want to do that are quiet and creative that you'll get around to later? Mercury retrograde is officially "later." Remember the "re"—review, rewrite, reflect, reconsider—and retrograde will reveal what you need to help you on your journey.

December/January

28 Monday
2nd ♉
☽ v/c 12:54 pm
☽ enters ♊ 8:13 pm
Color: Silver

Nutmeg enhances psychic powers and subtle senses

29 Tuesday
1st ♊
Color: White

For control, use bayberry incense or wax

30 Wednesday
2nd ♊
☽ v/c 3:29 pm
☽ enters ♋ 9:45 pm
Color: Yellow

31 Thursday
2nd ♋
Full Moon 2:13 pm
Color: Green

Healing period 10pm

New Year's Eve

1 Friday
3rd ♋
☽ v/c 10:43 am
☽ enters ♌ 9:41 pm
Color: Coral

New Year's Day
Kwanzaa ends
Birthday of Sir James Frazer,
author of *The Golden Bough*, 1854

2 Saturday

3rd ♌
Color: Gray

3 Sunday

3rd ♌
☽ v/c 4:55 pm
⛢ ℞ 7:12 pm
☽ enters ♍ 9:52 pm
Color: Orange

Death of Edgar Cayce, psychic, 1945

January

4 Monday

3rd ♍
Color: White

Snow – Work

Monday evening and night heavy snow fall

Aquarian Tabernacle Church registered in Australia by Lady Tamara Von Forslun, 1994

5 Tuesday

3rd ♍
☽ v/c 12:25 pm
☽ enters ♎ 11:58 pm
Color: Red

Eva Rang - Suggest arranging to meet with Terry

Snow sticking road (Br Brow) covered in snow

6 Wednesday

3rd ♎
Color: White

Freezing

Twelfth Night/Epiphany

Patricia Crowther's witchcraft radio show, *A Spell of Witchcraft*, airs in Britain, 1971

☽ Thursday

3rd ♎
4th quarter 5:40 am
Color: Crimson

Freezing

8 Friday

4th ♎
☽ v/c 1:07 am
☽ enters ♏ 5:00 am
Color: Purple

Freezing

Birthday of MacGregor Mathers, one of the three original founders of the Golden Dawn, 1854

Death of Dion Fortune, 1946

Set in Eastern Standard Time (EST)

Birch

The Celtic Tree Calendar is a lunar one based upon the Celtic Ogham letters and their tree correspondences. Birch corresponds with the Ogham letter *beth* (beeth), which speaks of new beginnings and fresh starts and growth. This is the perfect time to cast off the old and make way for the new. We begin 2010 under the blessings of the birch tree, one of the first trees appearing on bare soil after land has been cleared. Birch is known as a

"nursery tree," it nurtures others so that they may grow. Invite the spirit of birch to bless this year by lighting a white candle and placing it before a piece of birch bark or a picture of a birch tree. Feel the power of the birch growing from the ashes of the past year. Feel your potential for growth and focus on your goals. Repeat the following:

Sweetest birch, lovely tree of white,
I leave what I don't need behind
Spirit of birch bring me beginnings anew
Sending your blessings to all that I do.

—Mickie Mueller

---

9 Saturday

4th ♏
Color: Brown

Woke up with a runny nose - it dripped all day. Very cold. Damon slept.

Jamie Dodge wins lawsuit against the Salvation Army, which fired her based on her Wiccan religion, 1989

---

10 Sunday

4th ♏
☽ v/c 10:02 am
☽ enters ♐ 1:10 pm
Color: Amber

January

11 Monday
4th ♐
Color: Ivory

12 Tuesday
4th ♐
☽ v/c 9:43 pm
☽ enters ♑ 11:54 pm
Color: Black

Mary Smith hanged in England;
she had quarreled with neighbors,
who said that the Devil appeared
to her as a black man, 1616

13 Wednesday
4th ♑
♄ ℞ 10:56 am
Color: Brown

Final witchcraft laws
repealed in Austria, 1787

14 Thursday
4th ♑
Color: Green

Official Confession of Error by
jurors of Salem Witch Trials, 1696

Human Be-In, a Pagan-style festival,
takes place in San Francisco, attended by
Timothy Leary and Allen Ginsburg, 1967

☽ Friday
4th ♑
New Moon 2:11 am
☽ v/c 4:02 am
☿ D 11:52 am
☽ enters ♒ 12:17 pm
Color: Rose

Solar eclipse 2:07 am, 25° ♑ 02'

Set in Eastern Standard Time (EST)

---

16 Saturday

1st ≈
Color: Blue

---

17 Sunday

1st ≈
☽ v/c 3:22 pm
♃ enters ♓ 9:10 pm
Color: Gold

January

18 Monday

1st ♒

☽ enters ♓ 1:17 am
♀ enters ♒ 9:35 am
Color: Silver

Birthday of Martin Luther King, Jr. (observed)

19 Tuesday

1st ♓

☉ enters ♒ 11:28 pm
Color: White

Sun enters Aquarius
Birthday of Dorothy Clutterbuck,
who initiated Gerald Gardner, 1880

20 Wednesday

1st ♓

☽ v/c 1:06 am
☽ enters ♈ 1:36 pm
Color: Topaz

21 Thursday

1st ♈
Color: Purple

Celtic Tree Month of Rowan begins

22 Friday

1st ♈

☽ v/c 2:46 pm
☽ enters ♉ 11:39 pm
Color: Pink

Set in Eastern Standard Time (EST)

Lamb Pasties

½ cup onion, chopped
1 lb. lamb, ground
1 cup potatoes, diced
5 fresh mint leaves, chopped fine
1 T. garam masala
1 oz. organic gravy mix (1 package)
1 cup frozen peas
2 T. Worcestershire sauce
Salt and pepper to taste
9 oz. pastry mix (per 2-crust pie)
2 eggs, beaten

Combine onion and ground lamb in a frying pan with a bit of olive oil. Cook over medium heat until onions are translucent and meat is no longer pink. Add potatoes, mint leaves, garam marsala, and 1 cup water, then cook until potatoes are done. Mix in a packet of organic gravy mix and bring to a bubble on medium heat until thick. Remove from heat. Add frozen peas and Worcestershire sauce. Add salt and pepper, then remove from heat until cool. Roll out pastry into saucer-sized rounds. Place three heaping teaspoons of mixture in middle of each round. Moisten outside edge and then fold over to seal. Brush the beaten eggs on top of pasties. Bake pasties in a preheated 350 degree F oven for 15 minutes, or until pastry is golden.

—Nancy V. Bennett

◑ Saturday
1st ♉
2nd quarter 5:53 am
Color: Black

handwritten notes:
News ±
55 - 4·20 -445
555 - 4·43
55 - 5·20

Druid - Lancaster
every ½ hr 555 & 55
555 - 20 min even Hr
55 50 min even Hr
Stand 15

Cattle, horses, ants, gophers, moles, and bears are creatures of the Earth

24 Sunday
2nd ♉
☽ v/c 10:03 pm
Color: Orange

Wearing red promotes courage and willpower

25 Monday

2nd ♉
☽ enters ♊ 6:11 am
Color: Gray

Birthday of Robert Burns, Scottish poet, 1759

26 Tuesday

2nd ♊
Color: Maroon

27 Wednesday

2nd ♊
☽ v/c 1:32 am
☽ enters ♋ 9:01 am
Color: Brown

*Earth rules the magic of trees,
magnets, knots, and bindings*

28 Thursday

2nd ♋
☽ v/c 11:49 pm
Color: White

*The woodsy smell of oakmoss
connects with prosperity and fertility*

29 Friday

2nd ♋
☽ enters ♌ 9:10 am
Color: Purple

The Cold Moon

Many Native American tribes name the months or "Moons" based on important local natural events. To the Cherokee, January is the Cold Moon. Fierce northern air howls down to strip the heat from the world. To the Choctaw, this is the Cooking Moon. Dried fruits, vegetables, and meat from storage help the tribe survive the winter, but they take a long time to cook. To the Dakota Sioux, this is the Moon of the Terrible. Not only can winters on the plains be devastating, but many legends relate dire events—and this is a time of year for telling stories.

January is the peak of winter. The nights are long and dark. The weather is harsh and cold. Honor this time by working with its quiet, introspective energy. Now is a good time to make warm winter clothes if you knit, crochet, or sew. Cook foods that take a long time to prepare, such as soups and slow-cooker recipes or bake winter root vegetables such as potatoes and turnips. Large meat dishes such as ham and turkey are also appropriate.

For ritual themes, consider the home and hearth. Tell stories to create the framework of a ritual or to socialize afterwards.

—Elizabeth Barrette

☺ Saturday

2nd ♌
Full Moon 1:18 am
Color: Indigo

Cold Moon
Birthday of Zsuzsanna E. Budapest, feminist Witch

---

31 Sunday

3rd ♌
☽ v/c 1:27 am
☽ enters ♍ 8:23 am
Color: Yellow

Dr. Fian, believed to be the head of the North Berwick Witches, found guilty and executed for witchcraft in Scotland by personal order of King James VI (James I of England), 1591

February

1 Monday
3rd ♍
☽ v/c 11:17 pm
Color: Gray

2 Tuesday
3rd ♍
☽ enters ♎ 8:42 am
Color: Black

Imbolc
Groundhog Day
Leo Martello becomes a third-degree
Welsh traditionalist, 1973

3 Wednesday
3rd ♎
Color: Yellow

4 Thursday
3rd ♎
☽ v/c 4:27 am
☽ enters ♏ 11:56 am
Color: Green

Imbolc crossquarter day
(Sun reaches 15° Aquarius)

◑ Friday
3rd ♏
4th quarter 6:48 pm
Color: White

Earth tools include pentacles, plates, altars, and stones

Set in Eastern Standard Time (EST)

Imbolc

Imbolc is the time when things stir beneath the surface. It is the time of infinite possibilities for the new cycle of life and creativity, when energies are still gathering in the astral, preparing to manifest. The celebration is sacred to Brigid, goddess of smithcraft, poetry, and healing. Take time to concentrate on what you wish to manifest in the coming year. What needs craftwork applied to it, on any level? Can you sing or write it into  existence? Does any healing need to happen in your life?

Decorate your altar in red and white. Place a bowl of white roses in the center, flanked by red candles. Write a poem dedicated to Brigid. Don't worry, it doesn't need to rhyme—it only needs to be from the heart! Take a specially painted and prepared pot of earth and place several seeds in it. Let each seed represent something you wish to manifest. Honor and nurture these seedlings. Take a glass bowl filled with clean water and a handful of small, clear crystals. Name each crystal for something in your life that needs to be healed and drop them one by one into the bowl. As each healing occurs, remove that crystal. When the bowl is empty, pour away the water.

—Cerridwen Iris Shea

6 Saturday

4th ♏
☽ v/c 11:11 am
☽ enters ♐ 7:04 pm
Color: Black

7 Sunday

4th ♐
Color: Orange

Death of Thomas Aquinas, scholar who wrote that heresy was a product of ignorance and therefore criminal, and who refuted the *Canon Episcopi*, 1274

February

8 Monday
4th ♐
☽ v/c 11:58 pm
Color: Lavender

Birthday of Susun Weed, owner of
Wise Woman Publishing

Birthday of Evangeline Adams,
American astrologer, 1868

9 Tuesday
4th ♐
☽ enters ♑ 5:43 am
Color: Red

10 Wednesday
4th ♑
☿ enters ♒ 4:06 am
Color: Brown

Zsuzsanna Budapest arrested and later
convicted for fortunetelling, 1975

11 Thursday
4th ♑
♀ enters ♓ 7:10 am
☽ v/c 7:39 am
☽ enters ♒ 6:24 pm
Color: Turquoise

PICK UP MUG FROM
TESCO WITH DAMO'S
FACE PRINTED ONTO IT

12 Friday
4th ♒
Color: Rose

Gerald Gardner, founder
of the Gardnerian tradition,
dies of heart failure, 1964

Rowan

An ever-watchful guardian, the rowan tree, which corresponds to the Ogham letter *luis* (lweesh), is a symbol of protection and defense. The Rowan tree is sacred to the goddess Brigid and is associated with dragon energy and fire. Rowan teaches us to be aware of our surroundings and not to allow ourselves to be tricked or enchanted, keeping our wits about us. You may harness the protection of rowan by placing any or all of the following in a small red pouch: rowan berries, bark, wood or leaves, or a picture of a rowan tree, picture of a dragon, red glass beads with a tiny black star painted on each one. Draw the luis symbol on the pouch and light a red candle. You can carry this pouch for protection or hang it high in your home, charging it first with the following chant:

> *Rowan bring your firelight,*
> *A psychic shield of power and might.*
> *I see any obstacle in my way,*
> *Avoiding trouble come what may.*

—Mickie Mueller

☽ Saturday

4th ≈
New Moon 9:51 pm
☽ v/c 11:33 pm
Color: Blue

To spice up a relationship
and enhance sexual attraction, use clove oil

---

14 Sunday

1st ≈
☽ enters ♓ 7:23 am
Color: Gold

Valentine's Day
Chinese New Year (tiger)
Elsie Blum, a farmhand from
Oberstedten, Germany, sentenced
to death for witchcraft, 1652

February

15 Monday

1st ♓
♅ enters ♌ 10:46 pm
Color: Silver

Presidents' Day (observed)
Pope Leo X issues papal bull to ensure that
the secular courts carry out executions
of Witches convicted by the Inquisition,
1521; the bull was a response to the courts'
refusal to carry out the work of the Church

16 Tuesday

1st ♓
☽ v/c 9:32 am
☽ enters ♈ 7:30 pm
Color: Scarlet

Mardi Gras (Fat Tuesday)

17 Wednesday

1st ♈
Color: Topaz

Ash Wednesday

18 Thursday

1st ♈
☉ enters ♓ 1:36 pm
☽ v/c 10:52 pm
Color: White

Sun enters Pisces
Celtic Tree Month of Ash begins

19 Friday

1st ♈
☽ enters ♉ 5:55 am
Color: Purple

Set in Eastern Standard Time (EST)

20 Saturday

1st ♉
Color: Gray

Society for Psychical Research,
devoted to paranormal research,
founded in London, 1882

○ Sunday

1st ♉
☽ v/c 7:15 am
☽ enters ♊ 1:47 pm
2nd quarter 7:42 pm
Color: Amber

Birthday of Patricia Telesco,
Wiccan author

Stewart Farrar initiated into
Alexandrian Wicca, 1970

Death of Theodore Parker Mills, 1996

February

22 Monday
2nd ♊
Color: White

Birthday of Sybil Leek, Wiccan author, 1922

23 Tuesday
2nd ♊
⚡ enters ♉ 6:46 am
☽ v/c 12:29 pm
☽ enters ♋ 6:29 pm
Color: Gray

Cypress incense helps deal with people
who are not dealing with their emotions

24 Wednesday
2nd ♋
Color: Yellow

25 Thursday
2nd ♋
☽ v/c 12:48 pm
☽ enters ♌ 8:08 pm
Color: Crimson

To represent the four elements,
place a staurolite stone on your altar

26 Friday
2nd ♌
Color: Pink

Set in Eastern Standard Time (EST)

Quickening Moon

To the Cherokee, February is the Bony Moon. In their southeastern territory, this historically marked the hungry time when people and animals grew lean. Similarly, the Choctaw call this the Little Famine Moon. To the Dakota Sioux, it is the Moon When Trees Pop. Out on the plains, it can get so cold that the moisture inside living wood freezes and the expanding ice causes tree trunks to burst.

Toward the end of winter, people and wildlife have used up much of their reserves, so be cautious and conservative if you find resources stretching thin. Conversely, if you have enough to share, look to help others. Donating to a food bank or cooking supper for a friend who's lost a job can soften the bite of this sharp Moon. Assist wildlife with rich foods, suet, corn, and fresh water. Check forecasts of extreme cold, and protect vulnerable plants if necessary. Trees are especially vulnerable if warm weather that makes the sap run is followed by severe cold.

Magically, create abundance via giveaways and gratitude for what you have. Pray for people experiencing famine and hardship; contribute to charities that aid them. Work spells of protection for the land and wildlife.

—Elizabeth Barrette

---

27 Saturday

2nd ♌
☽ v/c 3:15 pm
☽ enters ♍ 7:52 pm
Color: Black

Pope John XXII issues first papal bull to discuss the practice of witchcraft, 1318

Birthday of Rudolf Steiner, philosopher and father of the biodynamic farming movement, 1861

☺ Sunday

2nd ♍
Full Moon 11:38 am
Color: Gold

Purim
Quickening Moon

March

1 Monday

3rd ♍
☿ enters ♓ 8:28 am
☽ v/c 12:36 pm
☽ enters ♎ 7:31 pm
Color: Silver

Preliminary hearings in the
Salem Witch trials held, 1692
Birthday of the Golden Dawn, 1888
Covenant of the Goddess (COG) formed, 1975

2 Tuesday

3rd ♎
Color: Gray

In earth spells, bury objects, plant
seeds, or draw images in the sand

3 Wednesday

3rd ♎
☽ v/c 3:43 pm
☽ enters ♏ 9:11 pm
Color: Topaz

4 Thursday

3rd ♏
Color: White

Chariot
2 Pentacles } *Next 24hrs*
5 swords } *8:00 pm — 8:00 pm Fri*

Church of All Worlds incorporates in
Missouri, 1968, becoming the first Pagan
church to incorporate in the United States

5 Friday

3rd ♏
☽ v/c 11:32 pm
Color: Coral

Chariot
2 pentacles } *Next 24hrs*
5 swords

Set in Eastern Standard Time (EST)

Ash

The ash tree corresponds with the Ogham letter *nuin* (nee-uhn), which tells us it is time to take action and transform our situation. Ash is the hardwood used to make tool handles and baseball bats, and one of the woods the Celts used it to make spear handles. The ash tree represents the power to manifest change through decisive and powerful action. To work with the ash tree energy, use fine-grade sandpaper and gently sand off a

tiny amount from an old ball bat, hockey stick, or tool handle made of ash, and sprinkle the dust on a green or yellow tea light candle. While you may use any piece of ash, tools and sports equipment have that "getting things done" vibe. Carve the nuin symbol on the candle. Visualize yourself taking action toward your goal, facing every challenge with success, and repeat:

> *Tree of ash, grant me strength,*
> *Power mighty and strong.*
> *I overcome my obstacles,*
> *Taking action of my own.*

—Mickie Mueller

---

6 Saturday

3rd ♏
☽ enters ♐ 2:36 am
Color: Indigo

Birthday of Laurie Cabot, Wiccan author

☽ Sunday

3rd ♐
♀ enters ♈ 7:33 am
4th quarter 10:42 am
Color: Yellow

William Butler Yeats initiated
into the Isis-Urania Temple
of the Golden Dawn, 1890

March

8 Monday
4th ♐
☽ v/c 6:13 am
☽ enters ♑ 12:13 pm
Color: White

9 Tuesday
4th ♑
Color: Black

Elestial, a blend of smoky quartz, changes
confusion to clarity and breaks through illusion to truth

10 Wednesday
4th ♑
♂ D 12:09 pm
☽ v/c 4:59 pm
Color: Brown

Date recorded for first meeting of
Dr. John Dee and Edward Kelley, 1582

Dutch clairvoyant and psychic
healer Gerard Croiser born, 1909

11 Thursday
4th ♑
☽ enters ♒ 12:42 am
Color: Crimson

12 Friday
4th ♒
Color: Purple

Stewart Edward White, psychic
researcher, born, 1873; he later
became president of the
American Society for Psychical
Research in San Francisco

Naniamo Eggs

First layer
2 cups Oreo cookie crumbs
½ cup chopped pecans
½ cup brown sugar
½ cup melted butter

Combine ingredients, then mold into egg-sized balls. Place balls on a cookie sheet with wax paper. Refrigerate for one hour.

Second layer
2 cups icing sugar
1 cup custard powder (or a package of instant banana or lemon pudding)
½ cup softened butter

Dribble milk into this mixture to make a thick icing. Mold this around the eggs. Refrigerate for an hour.

Third layer
Melt 8 squares of semisweet chocolate in a double-boiler. Using 2 spoons, quickly dip the eggs into the chocolate to cover. Refrigerate until hard.

—Nancy V. Bennett

---

13 Saturday
4th ≈
☽ v/c 7:57 am
☽ enters ♓ 1:44 pm
Color: Black

Jasmine guards against theft and other harms

---

14 Sunday
4th ♓
♀ ℞ 8:38 am
Color: Yellow

Daylight Saving Time begins at 2 am

March

☽ Monday
4th ♓
New Moon 5:01 pm
☽ v/c 8:01 pm
Color: Gray

Pete Pathfinder Davis becomes the first
Wiccan priest elected as president of the
Interfaith Council of Washington State, 1995

16 Tuesday
1st ♓
☽ enters ♈ 2:32 am
Color: Maroon

17 Wednesday
1st ♈
☿ enters ♈ 12:12 pm
Color: White

St. Patrick's Day
Eleanor Shaw and Mary Phillips executed in
England for bewitching a woman
and her two children, 1705

18 Thursday
1st ♈
☽ v/c 7:23 am
☽ enters ♉ 12:29 pm
Color: Purple

Celtic Tree Month of Alder begins
Birthday of Edgar Cayce, psychic researcher, 1877

19 Friday
1st ♉
♃ enters ♑ 9:47 am
Color: Pink

Elizabethan statute against witchcraft
enacted, 1563; this statute was replaced in
1604 by a stricter one from King James I

Ostara

Ostara is the time of hope, joy, and expectation. The seeds planted at Imbolc are showing the first signs of new growth. The tender shoots still have so much potential for growth. It's the time to look forward toward a bright future. The earth awakens from its slumber, not just on the astral, but on the physical. What was only a thought at Imbolc becomes tangible at Ostara.

It is the equinox, the time of balance between the light and the dark, where the cycle is about to tip into the realm of the light, more and more each day until the Summer Solstice.

This is also a time to share good fortune. The tradition of decorating eggs can be as intricate as the Ukrainian art of pysanky, with elaborate designs filled with meaning, or as simple as eggs decorated with runes. Hard-boil the eggs. Once cooled, immerse them in bowls of seasonal colors (blue, green, pink, yellow). Once the color has set and dried, use paint or colored markers to adorn the eggs with runes such as Feoh (wealth, cattle), Gebo (gift), Wunjo (joy), and Sowilo (Sun). Distribute the eggs to family and friends, and eat the eggs to ingest the good wishes for the coming cycle.

—Cerridwen Iris Shea

20 Saturday
1st ♉
☉ enters ♈ 1:32 pm
☽ v/c 3:41 pm
☽ enters ♊ 8:28 pm
Color: Gray

Ostara/Spring Equinox
Sun enters Aries
International Astrology Day
Death of Lady Sheba, Wiccan author
of *The Book of Shadows*, 2002

21 Sunday
1st ♊
Color: Amber

Mandate of Henry VIII against witchcraft
enacted, 1542; repealed in 1547
Green Egg magazine founded, 1968

March

22 Monday
1st ♊
☽ v/c 9:49 pm
Color: Lavender

Pope Clement urged by Phillip IV
to suppress Templar order, 1311

◑ Tuesday
1st ♊
☽ enters ♋ 2:16 am
2nd quarter 7:00 am
Color: Red

24 Wednesday
2nd ♋
Color: Brown

Birthday of Alyson Hannigan, who played
Willow on *Buffy the Vampire Slayer*
Arrest of Florence Newton, one of the few
Witches burned in Ireland, 1661

25 Thursday
2nd ♋
☽ v/c 12:39 am
☽ enters ♌ 5:39 am
Color: Green

Pope Innocent III issues papal bull to
establish the Inquisition, 1199

26 Friday
2nd ♌
Color: Coral

Birthday of Joseph Campbell, author
and professor of mythology, 1910

Alder

The alder tree corresponds to the Ogham letter *fearn* (fair-n) and whispers to us of our inner teacher or oracle and supports the bridge to our subconscious. Used to make shields and associated with the Celtic hero and oracle Bran the Blessed, the alder tree can provide shelter from emotional influences, allowing you to see clearly things that you may have overlooked. You may ask the alder tree for inner spiritual guidance to a question.

Fill a glass with water and before you go to sleep, holding the glass of water before you, ask yourself the question. Keep a pen and paper handy to record your dream—when you awake, the answer to your question should be revealed. With your finger, trace the alder/fearn symbol over the glass, and drink the water after you hold it high. Repeat the following three times:

> *Alder tree, guide of might,*
> *grant me intuition on this night.*
> *Blessed Bran, alders trees kin,*
> *Show to me the sage within.*

—Mickie Mueller

---

27 Saturday
2nd ♌
☽ v/c 3:04 am
☽ enters ♍ 6:57 am
Color: Blue

---

28 Sunday
2nd ♍
Color: Orange

Palm Sunday
Scott Cunningham dies of
complications caused by AIDS, 1993

☺ Monday
2nd ♍
☽ v/c 2:55 am
☽ enters ♎ 7:21 am
Full Moon 10:25 pm
Color: Gray

Storm Moon

30 Tuesday
3rd ♎
Color: White

Passover begins

31 Wednesday

3rd ♎
☽ v/c 8:13 am
☽ enters ♏ 8:41 am
♀ enters ♉ 1:35 pm
Color: Yellow

Last Witch trial in Ireland,
held at Magee Island, 1711

1 Thursday

3rd ♏
Color: Green

April Fools' Day (All Fools' Day—Pagan)

2 Friday

3rd ♏
☽ v/c 8:54 am
☿ enters ♉ 9:06 am
☽ enters ♐ 12:53 pm
Color: Purple

Good Friday
Orthodox Good Friday

The Storm Moon

According to the Cherokee, March is the Windy Moon. As winter turns to spring, storms sweep in and high winds damage trees and homes. The Choctaw call this the Big Famine Moon as reserves have been exhausted, but the renewal of life has yet to produce new foods to eat. The Dakota Sioux call this the Moon When Eyes Are Sore from Bright Snow. On the plains, snow still falls, reflecting the strengthening light of the Sun.

March holds the transition between winter and spring, a turbulent time of both hope and danger. Keep a wary eye out for severe weather. On the first warm day, avoid the temptation to run out in light clothes. Instead, dress in layers so you can respond to rapidly changing conditions—you'll catch fewer colds. Watch for the first signs of returning life, and rake mulch away from spring flowers as they sprout. Offer food to wildlife as long as it's consumed; put out scraps of fabric or string when birds begin to build nests.

In ritual space, honor the quickening life in the world around you. Use its burgeoning energy to work magic to empower new projects—plant young trees, launch a life-oriented business, or explore educational opportunities.

—Elizabeth Barrette

---

3 Saturday

3rd ♐
Color: Brown

---

4 Sunday

3rd ♐
☽ v/c 4:57 pm
☽ enters ♑ 9:07 pm
Color: Amber

Easter
Orthodox Easter

April

5 Monday
3rd ♑
Color: Lavender

Trial of Alice Samuel, her
husband, and her daughter, who
were accused of bewitching the
wife of Sir Henry Cromwell and
several village children, 1593

○ Tuesday
3rd ♑
4th quarter 5:37 am
⚷ D 8:36 am
♇ Rx 10:34 pm
Color: Red

Passover ends

7 Wednesday
4th ♑
☽ v/c 4:18 am
☽ enters ♒ 8:51 am
♄ enters ♍ 2:51 pm
Color: White

Church of All Worlds founded, 1962
First Wiccan "tract" published
by Pete Pathfinder Davis, 1996

8 Thursday
4th ♒
Color: Turquoise

William Alexander Aynton initiated into the
Isis-Urania temple of the Golden
Dawn, 1896; he would later be called the
"Grand Old Man" of the Golden Dawn

9 Friday
4th ♒
☽ v/c 5:44 pm
☽ enters ♓ 9:48 pm
Color: Pink

Set in Eastern Daylight Time (EDT)

10 Saturday
4th ♓
Color: Gray

Birthday of Rev. Montague Summers,
orthodox scholar and author of
A History of Witchcraft and Demonology, 1880

11 Sunday
4th ♓
Color: Orange

Burning of Major Weir, Scottish "sorcerer" who confessed of
his own accord, 1670; some historians believe that the major
became delusional or senile because up until his confession
he had an excellent reputation and was a pillar of society

April

12 Monday

4th ♓
☽ v/c 8:51 am
☽ enters ♈ 9:31 am
Color: Silver

*Mountaintops, windy beaches, airports,
schools, and offices support the energy of air magic*

13 Tuesday

4th ♈
Color: Black

☽ Wednesday

4th ♈
New Moon 8:29 am
☽ v/c 3:23 pm
☽ enters ♉ 6:55 pm
Color: Yellow

Adoption of the Principles of
Wiccan Belief at "Witch Meet"
in St. Paul, Minnesota, 1974

15 Thursday

1st ♉
Color: Purple

Celtic Tree Month of Willow begins
Birthday of Elizabeth Montgomery,
who played Samantha on *Bewitched*, 1933

16 Friday

1st ♉
Color: White

Birthday of Margot Adler, author
of *Drawing Down the Moon*

Set in Eastern Daylight Time (EDT)

Willow

The willow tree corresponds to the Ogham letter *saille* (shail-uh). The willow tree's roots run deep with emotion and the powers of divination. The willow is heavily associated with the Moon and Goddess energy. You may ask the willow tree to charge and bless your divination tools, tarot deck, crystal ball, runes, ogham set, etc., during the month of the willow tree. Place your favorite divination tools in a small willow basket, available at  most craft stores. You can do this on any Monday evening. Take the basket outside and sit with it under a willow tree. Visualize the willow tree's energy pouring down over your divination tools, filling them with its Goddess power. When you feel it's done, thank the tree, leave a gift (e.g., a crystal, coin, fertilizer stick). Try this charm while enchanting your tools:

> *Willow tree, lend your vibrations,*
> *Bless these tools of divination.*
> *And guide my heart that I may see,*
> *All they have to show to me.*

—Mickie Mueller

---

17 Saturday
1st ♉
☽ v/c 12:57 am
☽ enters ♊ 2:08 am
✷ enters ♊ 1:05 pm
Color: Blue

Aleister Crowley breaks into and takes over the Golden Dawn temple, providing the catalyst for the demise of the original Golden Dawn, 1900

---

18 Sunday
1st ♊
☿ ℞ 12:06 am
Color: Gold

When gambling, it is unlucky to sit cross-legged

April

19 Monday

1st ♊
☽ v/c 6:21 am
☽ enters ♋ 7:39 am
Color: Gray

Conviction of Witches
at second of four famous trials at
Chelmsford, England, 1579

20 Tuesday

1st ♋
☉ enters ♉ 12:30 am
☿ enters ♓ 2:37 am
Color: Scarlet

Sun enters Taurus

○ Wednesday

1st ♋
☽ v/c 10:07 am
☽ enters ♌ 11:42 am
2nd quarter 2:20 pm
Color: Topaz

22 Thursday

2nd ♌
Color: White

Earth Day; the first Earth Day was in 1970

23 Friday

2nd ♌
☽ v/c 11:35 am
☽ enters ♍ 2:24 pm
Color: Rose

The Wiccan pentacle is officially added to the
Veterans Administration's list of approved emblems
for memorials, markers, and gravestones, 2007

First National All-Woman Conference on
Women's Spirituality held, Boston, 1976

Set in Eastern Daylight Time (EDT)

Beltane

Beltane is the holiday of passion and purification. The heat of creation runs hot in the blood. It manifests in personal relationships, in the earth bursting forth with the fullness of its growth, and in creativity.

One tradition is to jump over the Beltane fire for purification. In outdoor urban rituals over the years, where it's been impossible to create a traditional, large bonfire, we've jumped the Sacred Grill. Take a small, tabletop grill and fire it up. Make sure the coals are glowing, but there's not a large flame. Toss some sacred herbs into the flames, such as sage, rosemary, cedar, etc. Place the grill on the ground within the sacred space, bless and consecrate it, and have the ritual participants carefully jump the Sacred Grill! The veil is almost as thin at Beltane as it is on Samhain. This is another good night to speak with the dead and perform acts of divination.

Sometimes singles feel depressed or excluded on Beltane because the focus is on passion, fertility, and couples. However, you can also be passionate about friends, family, one's vocation, art, the conditions in the world. Focus that passion and send it forth to make the world a better place.

—Cerridwen Iris Shea

---

24 Saturday
2nd ♍
Color: Brown

Flowers growing on a grave indicate that the person buried there has lived a good life

---

25 Sunday
2nd ♍
♀ enters ♊ 1:05 am
☽ v/c 2:21 pm
☽ enters ♎ 4:16 pm
Color: Amber

USA *Today* reports that Patricia Hutchins is the first military Wiccan granted religious leave for the sabbats, 1989

26 Monday
2nd ♎︎
Color: Silver

In air spells, use visualization, positive affirmations, fanning, or tossing objects

27 Tuesday
2nd ♎︎
☽ v/c 3:45 pm
☽ enters ♏︎ 6:28 pm
Color: White

☺ Wednesday
2nd ♏︎
Full Moon 8:19 am
♀ ℞ 7:01 pm
Color: Yellow

Wind Moon

29 Thursday
3rd ♏︎
☽ v/c 8:39 pm
☽ enters ♐︎ 10:36 pm
Color: Turquoise

Birthday of Ed Fitch, Wiccan author

30 Friday
3rd ♐︎
Color: Purple

Walpurgis Night; traditionally the German Witches gather on the Blocksberg, a mountain in northeastern Germany

Wind Moon

To the Cherokee, April is the Flower Moon. In the warm southeast, forests and meadows bloom with life and color. The Choctaw call this the Wildcat Moon. Lynxes and bobcats become more active. To the Dakota Sioux, this is the Moon When Geese Return in Scattered Formation. These dramatic birds migrating north mark the return of spring.

April bursts forth with new life. In warmer regions, it is time to plant crops and watch wild plants grow. Birds are nesting; animals often have young beside them. In colder climes, the warmth of spring is just arriving. As natural-food sources emerge, you can taper off most supplemental feeding for wildlife. Observe what animals and birds become active. Bring freshly picked flowers indoors to chase away the dullness of the cold season.

In ritual, this is a good time to honor plant and animal spirits. Work with flower totems and animals associated with spring such as rabbits, ducks, geese, cats, and sheep. Cast a circle with flowers, or do spells using the energy of flower seeds or bulbs that will help manifest your desire as the plants grow. Wish on a flock of flying geese to speed your dreams toward reality.

—Elizabeth Barrette

1 Saturday

3rd ♐
Color: Blue

Beltane/May Day
Order of the Illuminati formed in
Bavaria by Adam Weishaupt, 1776

2 Sunday

3rd ♐
☽ v/c 4:08 am
☽ enters ♑ 6:00 am
Color: Gold

A kitten born in May is said to be a Witch's cat

May

3 Monday

3rd ♑
Color: Gray

Birthday of D. J. Conway, Wiccan author

4 Tuesday

3rd ♑
☽ v/c 3:07 pm
☽ enters ♒ 4:52 pm
Color: Black

The *New York Herald Tribune*
carries the story of a woman who
brought her neighbor to court on
a charge of bewitchment, 1895

5 Wednesday

3rd ♒
Color: Brown

Cinco de Mayo
Beltane crossquarter day
(Sun reaches 15° Taurus)

◐ Thursday

3rd ♒
4th quarter 12:15 am
Color: Crimson

Long Island Church of Aphrodite
formed by Reverend Gleb Botkin, 1938

7 Friday

4th ♒
☽ v/c 2:36 am
☽ enters ♓ 5:34 am
Color: Purple

Set in Eastern Daylight Time (EDT)

Garlic Dip for Lovers

2 cups whole grain bread, cubed
1 T. balsamic vinegar
½ cup apple juice
½ cup water
¾ cup olive oil
1–3 cloves garlic, minced

Place above ingredients in a blender. Allow this to sit and soak for 10 minutes. Pulse briefly to combine.

½ cup fresh chives
7 fresh mint leaves
2–3 T. yogurt

Add the chives and mint leaves to the blender. Pulse to combine. Add yogurt and continue to pulse. Add more apple juice if needed to make a thick dip. Place in the refrigerator for at least an hour before serving.

Serve with bread toasts, pita triangles, and fresh veggies. For the true garlic lover, top with minced fresh garlic before serving. You can substitute garlic chives for the minced garlic. You can also substitute roasted garlic instead of fresh, for a less biting dip.

—Nancy V. Bennett

---

8 Saturday

4th ♓
Color: Brown

---

9 Sunday

4th ♓
☽ v/c 4:12 pm
☽ enters ♈ 5:29 pm
Color: Gold

Mother's Day
Joan of Arc canonized, 1920
First day of the Lemuria, a Roman festival of the dead; this
festival was probably borrowed from the Etruscans
and is one possible ancestor of our modern Halloween

May

10 Monday
4th ♈
Color: Lavender

Pearl balances erratic emotions
and helps in weathering cycles

11 Tuesday
4th ♈
☿ D 6:27 pm
Color: Red

Massachusetts Bay Colony Puritans
ban Christmas celebrations
because they are too Pagan, 1659

12 Wednesday
4th ♈
☽ v/c 12:11 am
☽ enters ♉ 2:48 am
Color: Topaz

☽ Thursday
4th ♉
New Moon 9:04 pm
Color: Purple

Celtic Tree Month of Hawthorn begins

14 Friday
1st ♉
☽ v/c 8:28 am
☽ enters ♊ 9:18 am
Color: Rose

Widow Robinson of Kidderminster
and her two daughters are arrested for
trying to prevent the return of Charles II
from exile by use of magic, 1660

Set in Eastern Daylight Time (EDT)

15 Saturday

1st ♊
Color: Gray

Air rules the magic of divination,
prophecy, and weather-watching

16 Sunday

1st ♊
☽ v/c 1:06 pm
☽ enters ♋ 1:46 pm
Color: Yellow

May

17 Monday
1st ♋
Color: White

18 Tuesday
1st ♋
☽ v/c 4:35 pm
☽ enters ♌ 5:06 pm
Color: Gray

Birds, insects, bats, flying squirrels,
and spiders are creatures of air

19 Wednesday
1st ♌
♀ enters ♋ 9:05 pm
Color: White

Shavuot

◑ Thursday
1st ♌
☽ v/c 7:43 pm
2nd quarter 7:43 pm
☽ enters ♍ 7:58 pm
☉ enters ♊ 11:34 pm
Color: Crimson

Sun enters Gemini

21 Friday
2nd ♍
Color: Coral

Birthday of Gwyddion Pendderwen,
Pagan bard, 1946

Set in Eastern Daylight Time (EDT)

Hawthorn

Surrounded by the blooming trees of spring, we brightly welcome the Celtic month of the hawthorn tree, which corresponds to the Ogham letter *huath* (hoo-ah) and teaches us to overcome tension and obstacles in our path. This small tree used in hedgerows is considered to be a guardian between the realms, and a protective, purifying tree. Often used in Beltane rituals, you may call on the hawthorn tree to remove obstacles to finding love during this lusty month. This is an outdoor spell. Gather a pink or lavender candle and some hawthorn blossoms (a picture is OK). At the end of this spell, scatter the blossoms to the wind or burn the picture and scatter the ashes. Over the next several weeks, keep your heart and eyes open for love on the horizon. When you are ready, light the candle and repeat:

Hawthorn tree of power this night,
Open my heart to love's delight,
Free my thoughts and cleanse my mind,
And help me find a true love mine.

—Mickie Mueller

22 Saturday

2nd ♍
☽ v/c 10:34 pm
☽ enters ♎ 10:50 pm
Color: Blue

Adoption of the Earth Religion
Anti-Abuse Act, 1988

23 Sunday

2nd ♎
Color: Orange

Pine is popular in cleaning supplies
because it really does cleanse and purify,
both on physical and metaphysical levels

May

24 Monday
2nd ♎
Color: Silver

*Gold stone in a belly chain or navel
ring protects the third chakra, aids
centering, and soothes stomach troubles*

25 Tuesday
2nd ♎
☽ v/c 12:01 am
☽ enters ♏ 2:17 am
Color: White

Scott Cunningham initiated into the
Traditional Gwyddonic Order of the Wicca, 1981

26 Wednesday
2nd ♏
❦ enters ♍ 10:50 am
Color: Brown

☺ Thursday
2nd ♏
☽ v/c 7:13 am
☽ enters ♐ 7:15 am
Full Moon 7:07 pm
♅ enters ♈ 9:44 pm
Color: Turquoise

Flower Moon
Birthday of Morning Glory
Zell-Ravenheart, Church of All Worlds
Final confession of witchcraft by
Isobel Gowdie, Scotland, 1662

28 Friday
3rd ♐
Color: White

Set in Eastern Daylight Time (EDT)

Flower Moon

In Cherokee tradition, May is the Planting Moon. In most temperate climates, the soil is warm enough for tender seedlings and seeds to prosper in the gentle sun and rain. The Choctaw call this the Panther Moon for the big cats native to the land. To the Dakota Sioux, this is the Moon When Leaves Are Green. Grass grows vigorously on the prairies; in forests and along river-banks, trees unfurl their leaves.

Plants and animals put out a burst of energy in the mild weather between winter's cold and summer's heat. This is a peak gardening month for many. The earliest crops that grow in late winter or early spring—such as asparagus—deliver the season's first edibles. Many plants that yield summer crops have set their fruit. People also focus on exuberant outdoor pursuits. Picnics, parades, sports, and outdoor activities foster family and community bonds.

Magically, use this time to foster growth and expansion. Work hard and play hard. Store some of that energy in magical artifacts. Gardeners bless their crops and cast spells to repel hungry pests. Fill rituals with lively activities such as dancing, singing, and acting out myths in sacred theater.

—Elizabeth Barrette

29 Saturday

3rd ♐
☽ v/c 12:40 pm
☽ enters ♑ 2:44 pm
Color: Brown

Air tools include the athame, sword, and censer

30 Sunday

3rd ♑
♄ D 2:09 pm
Color: Yellow

Death of Joan of Arc, 1431

May/June

31 Monday

3rd ♑
Ψ Rx 2:48 pm
☽ v/c 11:41 pm
Color: Lavender

Memorial Day (observed)

1 Tuesday

3rd ♑
☽ enters ♒ 1:08 am
Color: Black

Witchcraft Act of 1563
takes effect in England

2 Wednesday

3rd ♒
Color: Yellow

Birthday of Alessandro
di Cagliostro, magician, 1743

3 Thursday

3rd ♒
☽ v/c 10:56 am
☽ enters ♓ 1:34 pm
Color: White

◖ Friday

3rd ♓
⚷ Rx 3:04 am
4th quarter 6:13 pm
Color: Coral

If your clothes get caught on a briar branch,
you will have good luck involving money

Set in Eastern Daylight Time (EDT)

5 Saturday
4th ♓
Color: Brown

6 Sunday
4th ♓
☽ v/c 1:49 am
☽ enters ♈ 1:50 am
♃ enters ♈ 2:28 am
Color: Amber

June

7 Monday
4th ♈
♂ enters ♍ 2:11 am
♀ enters ♐ 2:24 pm
Color: White

*Dill arouses both physical lust and
emotional love, making dill pickles
perfect for a romantic picnic*

8 Tuesday
4th ♈
☽ v/c 9:13 am
☽ enters ♉ 11:41 am
⚹ enters ♋ 5:08 pm
Color: Gray

9 Wednesday
4th ♉
Color: Brown

*Birthday of Grace Cook, medium and
founder of the White Eagle Lodge, 1892*

10 Thursday
4th ♉
☿ enters ♊ 1:41 am
☽ v/c 3:50 pm
☽ enters ♊ 6:11 pm
Color: Turquoise

Celtic Tree Month of Oak begins

*Hanging of Bridget Bishop, first to
die in the Salem Witch trials, 1692*

11 Friday
4th ♊
Color: Rose

Wear an obsidian ring for grounding and protection

First Berries Pudding

2 cups seasonal berries (salmonberries,
   strawberries, raspberries, and
   thawed blackberries from last fall)
1 cup brown sugar
9 slices bread (no crusts)

Set aside ½ cup berries that are the
nicest looking. To the rest, add brown
sugar and crush the berries. Leave to
sit for 30 minutes.
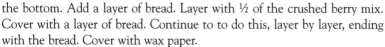

   Meanwhile take a nice glass bowl
and place the ½ cup of nice berries in
the bottom. Add a layer of bread. Layer with ½ of the crushed berry mix.
Cover with a layer of bread. Continue to to do this, layer by layer, ending
with the bread. Cover with wax paper.

   Place a plate on top of the mixture (I use a teacup saucer), and then
a small bowl filled with something heavy on top of that. Leave this for at
least 6 hours in your fridge.

   To serve, remove the plate and wax paper. Hold a large plate onto the
bowl and flip it over. With luck you should have a nice dome-shaped pudding, but it will taste good regardless of form. Serve with whipped cream
or vanilla ice cream and celebrate the solstice.

—Nancy V. Bennett

☽ Saturday
4th ♊
New Moon 7:15 am
☽ v/c 7:35 pm
☽ enters ♋ 9:50 pm
Color: Blue

13 Sunday
1st ♋
Color: Orange

Birthday of William Butler Yeats, poet and
member of the Golden Dawn, 1865
Birthday of Gerald Gardner, founder
of the Gardnerian tradition, 1884

June

14 Monday

1st ♋
♀ enters ♌ 4:50 am
☽ v/c 8:38 pm
☽ enters ♌ 11:54 pm
Color: Lavender

Flag Day

15 Tuesday

1st ♌
Color: Black

Margaret Jones becomes the first person executed
as a Witch in the Massachusetts Bay Colony,
1648; she was a Boston doctor who was accused of
witchcraft after several of her patients died

16 Wednesday

1st ♌
☽ v/c 11:24 pm
Color: Brown

17 Thursday

1st ♌
☽ enters ♍ 1:41 am
Color: White

Birthday of Starhawk, Wiccan author

18 Friday

1st ♍
Color: Pink

Church of All Worlds
chartered with the IRS, 1970

Summer Solstice

The Summer Solstice is a combination of joyous celebration and the realization that the wheel has reached a pinnacle and is now turning toward the dark again. It's a time to gather loved ones close and to celebrate community. If covens have hived off during the year, the Summer Solstice is the time for them all to gather with the original coven.

Participating in a large celebration is one of the joys of the Summer Solstice. Whether it's a group of covens reconnecting, a family reunion, or a neighborhood block party, the spirit of the community is paramount. Sharing food, experiences, and games contributes to bonds. Making a tub of potato salad or batch of brownies enhances the festivity of solstice.

And yet, a few quiet moments in a darkened room with a lit candle, honoring the fact that after today, the wheel has turned and the light will fractionally shorten every day, will give you a sense of peace. It is a time for inner connection as well, because the inner and outer communities are interwoven. That can be represented with the brightly colored woven placemats so popular during this season!

—Cerridwen Iris Shea

○ Saturday

1st ♍
2nd quarter 12:30 am
☽ v/c 1:04 am
☽ enters ♎ 4:13 am
Color: Gray

Fire rules the magic of candles, stars, and time

20 Sunday

2nd ♎
Color: Gold

Father's Day

June

21 Monday

2nd ♎︎
☽ v/c 5:44 am
☉ enters ♋︎ 7:28 am
☽ enters ♏︎ 8:14 am
Color: Silver

Sun enters Cancer
Midsummer/Litha/Summer Solstice

22 Tuesday

2nd ♏︎
Color: White

Final witchcraft law in
England repealed, 1951

23 Wednesday

2nd ♏︎
☽ v/c 11:32 am
☽ enters ♐︎ 2:10 pm
Color: Topaz

24 Thursday

2nd ♐︎
♀ D 10:28 am
Color: Purple

Birthday of Janet Farrar, Wiccan author
James I Witchcraft Statute of 1604 is
replaced in 1763 with a law against
pretending to practice divination and
witchcraft; law stands until 1951

25 Friday

2nd ♐︎
☿ enters ♋︎ 6:32 am
☽ v/c 7:33 pm
☽ enters ♑︎ 10:21 pm
Color: Pink

A law is introduced in Germany by
Archbishop Siegfried III to encourage
conversion rather than burning of heretics, 1233

Set in Eastern Daylight Time (EDT)

Strong Sun Moon

June is the Green Corn Moon. Corn is a vital crop in Cherokee culture. At this time, its green stalks grow quickly and put out their tassels. The Choctaw call this the Windy Moon—likely a reference to the summer thunderstorms that can spawn tornado activity. This is the Moon When Juneberries Are Ripe for the Dakota Sioux, mainly hunter-gatherers who kept close tabs on ripening times.

June brings a world full of exuberant green energy. Both domestic and wild foods flourish. Corn remains a staple crop today. Many different berries and other soft fruits begin to ripen in June: juneberries, strawberries, mulberries, raspberries, and cherries. Yet the tempestuous weather of early summer makes it prudent to keep an eye on the sky. Take advantage of the long days to garden or work outdoors.

Honor this season with celebrations of the Sun and of gardening. Do spells and rituals tied to the abundance of staple crops such as corn and their respective deities. If you don't have a garden, visit a "you pick" berry farm to experience the effort—and enjoyment—of gathering your own food, much as your ancestors did. Be prepared to protect against violent storms.

—Elizabeth Barrette

☺ **Saturday**

2nd ♑

Full Moon 7:30 am

Color: Indigo

Strong Sun Moon

Lunar eclipse 7:38 am, 4° ♑ 50'

Birthday of Stewart Farrar, Wiccan author

Richard of Gloucester assumes the English throne after accusing the widowed queen of Edward IV of witchcraft, 1483

---

27 **Sunday**

3rd ♑

Color: Yellow

Birthday of Scott Cunningham, Wiccan author, 1956

June/July

28 Monday
3rd ♑
☽ v/c 5:56 am
☽ enters ♒ 8:52 am
Color: Gray

Dragons, lions, bees, scorpions,
phoenixes, and coyotes are creatures of fire

29 Tuesday
3rd ♒
Color: Red

30 Wednesday
3rd ♒
☽ v/c 6:03 pm
☽ enters ♓ 9:10 pm
Color: White

Clove incense connects with solar energy

1 Thursday
3rd ♓
Color: Green

It is unlucky to use real flowers, real food,
or real money in a theatrical performance

2 Friday
3rd ♓
Color: Coral

Oak

The oak tree corresponds with the Ogham letter *duir* (doo-er) and is a symbol of strength and endurance, becoming a powerful spiritual symbol to the Celts. The oak month is the end of the reign of the Oak King—a good time to cast off the old and welcome the new. This month you may contact the dryads of the oak to guide you through the doorway of change, embracing your inner strength. Surround a green candle

with oak leaves and acorns or other oak tree representation. When you commune with the oak, write any messages you receive while in the other realm to further ponder. In this spell, visualize a mighty oak tree with a magical door opening in the trunk. You will step inside and feel the power of the oak fill you. Begin by lighting the candle, then repeat three times:

> *By mighty oak, this time of change,*
> *My fears for strength I now exchange.*
> *As now I step beyond the door,*
> *I find the power within my core.*

—Mickie Mueller

---

3 Saturday

3rd ♓︎
☽ v/c 7:17 am
☽ enters ♈︎ 9:44 am
Color: Blue

Trial of Joan Prentice, who was accused of sending an imp in the form of a ferret to bite children; she allegedly had two imps named Jack and Jill, 1549

☽ Sunday

3rd ♈︎
4th quarter 10:35 am
Color: Yellow

Independence Day

July

5 Monday

4th ♈
♅ ℞ 12:50 pm
☽ v/c 5:24 pm
☽ enters ♉ 8:29 pm
Color: Ivory

Conviction of Witches at third of four
famous trials at Chelmsford, England, 1589

6 Tuesday

4th ♉
Color: Maroon

Scott Cunningham is initiated into
Ancient Pictish Gaelic Way, 1981

7 Wednesday

4th ♉
Color: White

8 Thursday

4th ♉
☽ v/c 2:10 am
☽ enters ♊ 3:51 am
Color: Turquoise

Celtic Tree Month of Holly begins

9 Friday

4th ♊
☿ enters ♌ 12:29 pm
Color: Pink

Death of Herman Slater,
proprietor of Magickal Childe
bookstore in New York, 1992
Birthday of Amber K, Wiccan author

10 Saturday

4th ♊
☽ v/c 6:17 am
♀ enters ♍ 7:32 am
☽ enters ♋ 7:38 am
Color: Indigo

☽ Sunday

4th ♋
New Moon 3:40 pm
Color: Gold

Solar eclipse 3:33 pm, 19° ♋ 24'

July

12 Monday
1st ♋
☽ v/c 7:48 am
☽ enters ♌ 8:53 am
Color: Lavender

Vanilla attracts men; serve vanilla ice
cream topped with romantic fruit
such as strawberries to your sweetheart

13 Tuesday
1st ♌
Color: Red

Birthday of Dr. John Dee, magician, 1527

14 Wednesday
1st ♌
☽ v/c 6:23 am
☽ enters ♍ 9:15 am
Color: Yellow

First crop circles recorded
on Silbury Hill, 1988

15 Thursday
1st ♍
Color: Crimson

16 Friday
1st ♍
☽ v/c 9:46 am
☽ enters ♎ 10:24 am
Color: White

Deserts, volcanoes, athletic fields, fireplaces,
ovens, and bedrooms intensify fire magic

Set in Eastern Daylight Time (EDT)

Holly

You have built up strength during the Oak month, and now you may test your steel and valor. Holly corresponds with the Ogham letter *tinne* (chin-yuh), speaking of the strength gained by a challenge. Holly was hardened in flames and used as spears—it was said that when heated, holly would become strong as iron. If you wish to grow stronger from everyday challenges and overcome them, enlist the help of the holly spirit. As  you gaze into the candle's flame, feel it filling you. It blesses you with the ability to face any challenge in your path with insight and strength. You can overcome anything, and you'll come away stronger than before.

Gather a few holly leaves (or another symbol of holly) and a green candle. Carve the tinne/holly symbol on the candle and light it, saying:

I salute the blessed holly tree,
In justice's name I do decree,
As every challenge comes my way,
The flame will temper my swordplay.

—Mickie Mueller

---

17 Saturday

1st ♎
Color: Black

First airing of *The Witching Hour*, a Pagan radio show hosted by Winter Wren and Don Lewis, on station WONX in Evanston, Illinois, 1992

○ Sunday

1st ♎
2nd quarter 6:11 am
☽ v/c 10:26 am
☽ enters ♏ 1:42 pm
Color: Orange

July

19 Monday
2nd ♏
Color: Gray

Rebecca Nurse hanged in
Salem, Massachusetts, 1692

20 Tuesday
2nd ♏
☿ enters ♒ 5:36 am
☽ v/c 7:43 pm
☽ enters ♐ 7:48 pm
Color: Scarlet

Pope Adrian VI issues a papal bull to the
Inquisition to re-emphasize the 1503
bull of Julius II calling for the purging
of "sorcerers by fire and sword," 1523

21 Wednesday
2nd ♐
♄ enters ♎ 11:10 am
Color: White

22 Thursday
2nd ♐
☉ enters ♌ 6:21 pm
Color: Green

Sun enters Leo
Northamptonshire Witches
condemned, 1612
First modern recorded sighting
of the Loch Nesss monster, 1930

23 Friday
2nd ♐
☽ v/c 12:50 am
☽ enters ♑ 4:39 am
♃ ℞ 8:03 am
Color: Rose

Set in Eastern Daylight Time (EDT)

Blessing Moon

In Cherokee tradition, July is the Ripe Corn Moon. First sweet corn and then dent corn ripen for harvest. As a staple food and sacred material, corn attracts much attention throughout its life cycle. To the Choctaw, this is the Crane Moon, recognizing these large water birds. The Dakota Sioux call this the Moon of the Middle Summer. Indeed, for much of America, so it is: the three hottest months are June, July, and August.

July brings a swell of new foods: corn and tomatoes are ripening, along with many vine fruits such as squash and cucumbers. Visit your local farmers' market to enjoy fresh seasonal produce. Watch birds and other animals raising their young. But be careful. While the Sun passed its peak at the solstice, the heat is still increasing. Respect the Sun's power; avoid direct midday sunlight and excess exposure.

Rituals in July may celebrate staple crops such as corn or supporting crops such as squash—whatever ripens in your area at this time. Rituals to honor the Sun, light, heat, fire, and so forth are also appropriate. Magically, tap into the rich power of the Sun to fuel spells for success and prosperity.

—Elizabeth Barrette

24 Saturday
2nd ♑
Color: Brown

☺ Sunday
2nd ♑
☽ v/c 10:20 am
☽ enters ♒ 3:38 pm
Full Moon 9:37 pm
Color: Amber

Blessing Moon
Death of Pope Innocent VIII, who issued
bull *Summis Desiderantes Affectibus*, 1492

26 Monday

3rd ≈
Color: Silver

Confession of Chelmsford Witches at first of four famous trials at Chelmsford, 1566; the others were held in 1579, 1589, and 1645; "Witch Finder General" Matthew Hopkins presided at the 1645 trials

27 Tuesday

3rd ≈
☿ enters ♍ 5:43 pm
☽ v/c 11:46 pm
Color: Black

Jennet Preston becomes the first of the "Malkin Tower" Witches to be hung; she was convicted of hiring Witches to help her murder Thomas Lister, 1612

28 Wednesday

3rd ≈
☽ enters ♓ 4:00 am
Color: Brown

29 Thursday

3rd ♓
♂ enters ♎ 7:46 pm
☽ v/c 11:44 pm
Color: Purple

Agnes Waterhouse, one of the Chelmsford Witches, is hanged under the new witchcraft statute of Elizabeth I, 1566; she was accused of having a spotted cat familiar named Sathan

30 Friday

3rd ♓
☽ enters ♈ 4:42 pm
Color: White

Conrad of Marburg is murdered on the open road, presumably because he had shifted from persecuting poor heretics to nobles, 1233

Lughnasadh

The beginning of August heralds the first harvest, Lammas, Lughnasadh. Sacred to the Celtic Sun god Lugh, the man of many skills, this is a day to enjoy the first fruits of one's labors that began at Imbolc. Reflect on the story of Lugh's arrival at the gates of Tara. Tara accepted those with special skills. Every skill Lugh listed was already held by someone within the gates; but no one else embodied all—that's how he entered.

This first harvest is a time for celebration, for traditional games, and friendly competition. Spend time with friends and family, playing and celebrating in the joy of the outdoors and the still warmth of the summer Sun.

What skill have you acquired during this growth cycle? What do you need to celebrate? Is there anything you've done recently that needs to be cut away? Harvest is not only a time of gathering, but a time of cutting back. What do you need to cut back on or sacrifice in order to move forward?

Prepare your favorite cornbread recipe. Shape the loaf like a man. Bake it, slice off the head (a symbol of sacrifice), share it, and eat it to signify the duality of a bountiful harvest and the need for sacrifice.

—Cerridwen Iris Shea

---

31 Saturday
3rd ♈
Color: Blue

Birthday of H. P. Blavatsky, founder
of the Theosophical Society, 1831
Date of fabled meeting of British
Witches to raise cone of power to stop
Hitler's invasion of England, 1940

---

1 Sunday
3rd ♈
☽ v/c 11:54 pm
Color: Gold

Lammas/Lughnasadh
Birthday of Edward Kelley,
medium of Dr. John Dee, 1555
AURORA Network UK founded, 2000

August

2 Monday

3rd ♈
☽ enters ♉ 4:13 am
☿ enters ♌ 1:00 pm
Color: Gray

Birthday of Henry Steele Olcott,
who cofounded the Theosophical
Society with H. P. Blavatsky, 1832

○ Tuesday

3rd ♉
4th quarter 12:59 am
Color: Red

4 Wednesday

4th ♉
☽ v/c 8:44 am
☽ enters ♊ 12:54 pm
Color: Topaz

*For fire spells, burn objects
or pass them through flame or smoke*

5 Thursday

4th ♊
Color: Crimson

Celtic Tree Month of Hazel begins

6 Friday

4th ♊
☽ v/c 5:22 pm
☽ enters ♋ 5:50 pm
♀ enters ♎ 11:47 pm
Color: Purple

Set in Eastern Daylight Time (EDT)

Hunter's Hare

1 rabbit (or hare), cut into sections
(you may use chicken breasts,
thighs, and drumsticks)
Olive oil
1 cup mushrooms (wild or
portabello), sliced
½ cup flour
1 onion, cut into slices
1 red pepper, cut into slices
1 cup white wine
1 cup chicken stock (or water)
2 T. flour
2 T. sour cream

Dredge the rabbit sections in flour. In a large frying pan or Dutch oven, add some olive oil and brown the rabbit. Then add the onions and mushrooms and cook for a minute or two. Add the wine and enough chicken stock to cover the food. Bring to a boil, then reduce heat and cover. Simmer for an hour.

Combine the flour with sour cream. Stir into the dish to thicken sauce. Add salt and pepper to taste. Serve with a nice crusty bread and a fine ale. Drink the first toast to the hunters of our past and present.

—Nancy V. Bennett

7 Saturday

4th ♋
☽ v/c 2:46 pm
Color: Brown

Lammas crossquarter day
(Sun reaches 15° Leo)

8 Sunday

4th ♋
☿ D 2:31 pm
☽ enters ♌ 7:23 pm
Color: Gold

August

☽ Monday
4th ♌

⚴ enters ♎ 2:10 am
New Moon 11:08 pm
Color: White

10 Tuesday
1st ♌
☽ v/c 3:10 pm
☽ enters ♍ 7:01 pm
Color: Black

*Fire tools include knives, censers,
candles, lamps, and lighters*

11 Wednesday
1st ♍
☽ v/c 8:04 pm
Color: Topaz

Ramadan begins
Laurie Cabot withdraws from Salem,
Massachusetts, mayoral race, 1987
Birthday of Edain McCoy, Wiccan author

12 Thursday
1st ♍
☽ enters ♎ 6:43 pm
Color: Green

13 Friday
1st ♎
♅ enters ♓ 11:36 pm
Color: Pink

Aradia de Toscano allegedly
born in Volterra, Italy, 1313
Church of Wicca founded in Australia
by Lady Tamara Von Forslun, 1989

Set in Eastern Daylight Time (EDT)

14 Saturday

1st ♎︎
☽ v/c 4:06 pm
☽ enters ♏︎ 8:26 pm
Color: Gray

*Grapes promote fertility, whether
as wine, juice, jelly, or even raisins!*

15 Sunday

1st ♏︎
Color: Yellow

Birthday of Charles Godfrey Leland,
author of *Aradia, Gospel of Witches*, 1824

August

◐ Monday
1st ♏
2nd quarter 2:14 pm
Color: Silver

17 Tuesday
2nd ♏
☽ v/c 1:24 am
☽ enters ♐ 1:34 am
Color: Gray

Scott Cunningham's first
initiation into Wicca, 1973

18 Wednesday
2nd ♐
Color: Brown

Father Urbain Grandier found
guilty of bewitching nuns at a
convent in Loudoun, France, 1634

19 Thursday
2nd ♐
☽ v/c 9:58 am
☽ enters ♑ 10:17 am
Color: Purple

John Willard and Reverend
George Burroughs put to death
in the Salem Witch trials, 1692

20 Friday
2nd ♑
☿ ℞ 3:59 pm
Color: Coral

Execution of Lancashire Witches, 1612
Birthday of H. P. Lovecraft, horror
writer and alleged magician, 1890
Birthday of Ann Moura, author and Witch

Hazel

The hazel corresponds to the Ogham letter *coll* (cull) and is the bringer of enlightenment and inspiration. The legendary Salmon of Wisdom lived at the foot of the hazel and gained its powers from eating nine hazelnuts. Finn MacColl, in turn, gained gifts of insight from eating the salmon. To open the door for creative inspiration, why not enlist the help of the hazel tree during its month? Gather nine hazel nuts, a hazelnut-scented candle,  and small fabric bag. Carve the coll/hazel symbol on the candle and paint one on the bag. Light the candle and recite the following charm nine times, each time dropping a hazelnut in the bag. When you're done, tie the bag closed with nine knots, and keep it nearby when you are working on any project that could benefit from some added inspiration.

Hazel fair and blessed tree,
Hazel nuts smooth and lovely,
Awaken within me inspiration,
Creativity from life's cauldron.

—Mickie Mueller

21 Saturday
2nd ♑
☽ v/c 9:08 pm
☽ enters ♒ 9:37 pm
Color: Indigo

22 Sunday
2nd ♒
Color: Amber

Pope John XXII orders the Inquisition at Carcassonne to seize the property of Witches, sorcerers, and those who make wax images, 1320

August

23 Monday

2nd ≈
☉ enters ♍ 1:27 am
Color: Ivory

Sun enters Virgo

☺ Tuesday

2nd ≈
☽ v/c 4:29 am
☽ enters ♓ 10:11 am
Full Moon 1:05 pm
Color: Red

Corn Moon

25 Wednesday

3rd ♓
Color: Yellow

Sunflower helps discover the truth,
shedding light on secrets and mysteries

26 Thursday

3rd ♓
☽ v/c 10:00 pm
☽ enters ♈ 10:49 pm
Color: White

27 Friday

3rd ♈
Color: Purple

Mace incense captures the energy of Mercury

Set in Eastern Daylight Time (EDT)

Corn Moon

To the Cherokee, August is the Fruit Moon. Some cane berries have a second ripening period at this time. Many tree fruits also ripen in August including peaches, plums, and the earliest "dessert" apples. In Choctaw tradition, this is the Women's Moon, a time for feminine mysteries and ceremonies. The Dakota Sioux refer to this as the Moon When All Things Ripen. Most vegetables that haven't already matured begin to yield. Many wild plants also set their seeds and fruits. The early grains ripen too.

August marks the seasonal shift. Growth slows and changes focus from expansion to condensation as plants and animals prepare for the end of the growing season. Root crops store energy. Animals gorge on abundant food to put on fat for winter. People spend hours harvesting and preserving food.

Rituals in August may acknowledge it as the first of the harvest months, with September and October to follow. Some myths focus on sacrificed gods and grain gods, who die so that others may live. Magically, work spells for good weather and good harvests. Work to strengthen community ties in your coven or other magical/spiritual group.

—Elizabeth Barrette

28 Saturday
3rd ♈
Color: Black

It's not just for bugs anymore; citronella incense
banishes all undesirables and has a strong warding effect

29 Sunday
3rd ♈
☽ v/c 4:47 am
☽ enters ♉ 10:35 am
Color: Orange

Election of Pope Innocent VIII, who issued the
papal bull *Summis Desiderantes Affectibus*, 1484

30 Monday
3rd ♉
Color: Lavender

A good stone for teachers and healers
is kunzite as it aids compassion,
confidence, and emotional balance

31 Tuesday
3rd ♉
☽ v/c 7:13 pm
☽ enters ♊ 8:19 pm
Color: White

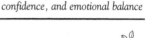

Birthday of Raymond Buckland,
who, along with his wife, Rosemary,
is generally credited with bringing
Gardnerian Wicca to the United States

○ Wednesday
3rd ♊
4th quarter 1:22 pm
Color: Brown

2 Thursday
4th ♊
Color: Purple

Celtic Tree Month of Vine begins
Birthday of Reverend Paul
Beyerl, Wiccan author

3 Friday
4th ♊
☽ v/c 1:40 am
☽ enters ♋ 2:50 am
Color: White

4 Saturday

4th ♋
Color: Blue

Lakes, streams, fountains, swimming pools,
bathrooms, and steam rooms empower water magic

5 Sunday

4th ♋
☽ v/c 4:31 am
☽ enters ♌ 5:45 am
Color: Amber

September

6 Monday
4th ♌
Color: Silver

Labor Day

7 Tuesday
4th ♌
☽ v/c 4:17 am
☽ enters ♍ 5:53 am
Color: Gray

Founding of the Theosophical
Society by H. P. Blavatsky, Henry
Steele Olcott, and others, 1875

☽ Wednesday
4th ♍
New Moon 6:30 am
♀ enters ♏ 11:44 am
Color: Yellow

Wear yellow when studying or taking tests

9 Thursday
1st ♍
♃ enters ♓ 12:50 am
☽ v/c 4:59 am
☽ enters ♎ 5:01 am
Color: Green

Rosh Hashanah

10 Friday
1st ♎
Color: Pink

Ramadan ends
Birthday of Carl Llewellyn
Weschcke, owner and president
of Llewellyn Worldwide

Set in Eastern Daylight Time (EDT)

Vine

Vine corresponds to the Ogham letter *muin* (muhn) and heralds the time of harvest and completion. Grapes, though not native to the Celtic regions, became embraced as the most important ingredient in winemaking, and are associated with the smiling, leafy Green Man. The fruits of the vine are integral to celebrations worldwide, and as our crops mature, why not celebrate your prosperity during the harvest season? Pour a glass of wine or grape juice and place it within a small grapevine wreath found at a craft store. Light any candle the color of the autumn leaves. List of all the good things you've harvested in your life this year. When you are done with this celebration, pour the remaining wine on the earth as an offering of thanks. Raise your glass and before you sip, repeat the following charm:

I raise my glass and make a toast,
The vine month brings a harvest to boast,
My gratefulness for the year's abundance,
I give my thanks with greatest reverence.

—Mickie Mueller

11 Saturday

1st ♎
☽ v/c 1:16 am
☽ enters ♏ 5:21 am
Color: Gray

Birthday of Silver RavenWolf,
Wiccan author

12 Sunday

1st ♏
☿ D 7:09 pm
Color: Gold

September

13 Monday
1st ♏
☽ v/c 7:53 am
☽ enters ♐ 8:52 am
Color: Lavender

Need to neutralize a sour disposition?
Grapefruit oil can help

14 Tuesday
1st ♐
♇ D 12:37 am
♂ enters ♏ 6:38 pm
Color: Red

Phillip IV of France draws up
the order for the arrest of
the French Templars, 1306

Birthday of Henry Cornelius Agrippa,
scholar and magician, 1486

○ Wednesday
1st ♐
2nd quarter 1:50 am
☽ v/c 2:52 pm
☽ enters ♑ 4:30 pm
Color: Topaz

16 Thursday
2nd ♑
Color: Green

Dolphins, seals, whales, otters, crabs,
fish, frogs, swans, ducks, water striders,
and dragonflies are water creatures

17 Friday
2nd ♑
Color: Purple

Bewitched debuts on ABC-TV, 1964

Set in Eastern Daylight Time (EDT)

Mabon

Mabon, the Autumn Equinox, is the counterbalance to Ostara. Once again, night and day are equal. Yet, after tonight, the seesaw tips toward night more than day.

The time of the second harvest, Mabon's another time to gather the fruits of one's labor and to cut away what is no longer necessary. It's a time to reflect on what fell out of balance, and how to right that balance to move into the dark portion of the year. A ritual performed with a small scale—where you write what's gotten out of balance and place it on one side, and write ideas on how to retrieve the balance and place it on the other—will guide you.

The Autumn Equinox is also known as the Witches' Thanksgiving. On the November holiday, you often travel to spend time with your family. Today, spend the day with the family you've created out of friends, colleagues, neighbors, and loved ones. Throw a large potluck feast. Celebrate outside if weather permits. Take a moment to remember those who were lost through the year, those who were harvested. Give thanks for all that is good in your life, and take a few minutes to share your gratitude with those gathered.

—Cerridwen Iris Shea

18 Saturday
2nd ♑
☽ v/c 1:13 am
☽ enters ♒ 3:35 am
Color: Brown

Yom Kippur

19 Sunday
2nd ♒
Color: Orange

September

20 Monday

2nd ≈
☽ v/c 9:09 am
☽ enters ♓ 4:15 pm
Color: White

21 Tuesday

2nd ♓
Color: White

Moldavite boosts psychic powers and channeling,
but also helps people feel at home here on Earth

22 Wednesday

2nd ♓
☉ enters ♎ 11:09 pm
Color: Brown

Mabon/Fall Equinox
Sun enters Libra

☺ Thursday

2nd ♓
☽ v/c 1:52 am
☽ enters ♈ 4:47 am
Full Moon 5:17 am
Color: Crimson

Harvest Moon
Sukkot begins

24 Friday

3rd ♈
Color: White

Harvest Moon

The Cherokee refer to September as the Nut Moon for the many nut trees that drop their fruit at this time—acorns, hickory nuts, walnuts, etc. These provide a rich food source for humans and wildlife. Hunters stake out a spot near a stand of nut trees hoping to find game animals that come to feed. To the Choctaw, this is the Mulberry Moon. Mulberries fruit during much of the summer, but some trees put out one last peak of fruit now. The Dakota Sioux call this the Moon When The Calves Grow Hair. On the plains, when the weather grows chilly, the young buffalo, elk, and other animals born earlier this year become shaggy and plump for the winter.

September marks a time when animals and people concentrate on stocking up for the cold season. The selection of fresh foods narrows; many ripening now will store well for a long time. Some baby animals are ready to leave their mothers. Wildlife crowds into stands of berries and nut trees.

Magically, this is a good time for spells of abundance, especially for saving money. Rituals may honor trees or tree deities. Spells for masculine power and virility are also timely; use seasonal nuts to represent male energy.

—Elizabeth Barrette

25 Saturday
3rd ♈
☽ v/c 9:12 am
☽ enters ♉ 4:17 pm
Color: Black

U.S. Senate passes an amendment (705) attached by Senator Jesse Helms to House Resolution 3036 (1986 budget bill), denying tax-exempt status to any organization that espouses satanism or witchcraft, 1985

26 Sunday
3rd ♉
Color: Yellow

Joan Wiliford hanged at Faversham, England, 1645; she testified that the Devil came to her in the form of a black dog that she called "Bunnie"

27 Monday
3rd ♉
☽ v/c 11:03 pm
Color: Gray

28 Tuesday
3rd ♉
☽ enters ♊ 2:10 am
Color: Scarlet

Water tools include chalices, cauldrons, spoons, and mirrors

29 Wednesday
3rd ♊
Color: White

Sukkot ends

○ Thursday
3rd ♊
☽ v/c 6:37 am
☽ enters ♋ 9:46 am
4th quarter 11:52 pm
Color: Turquoise

Celtic Tree Month of Ivy begins

1 Friday
4th ♋
Color: Pink

Birthday of Isaac Bonewits,
Druid, magician, and Witch
Birthday of Annie Besant,
Theosophical Society president, 1847

Three Sisters Chili

3 cups beans, (pinto, kidney,
    navy, garbanzo, etc.), precooked or
    canned (drained and rinsed)
Olive oil
1 red onion, sliced
2 cloves garlic, chopped
1 cup celery, chopped
2 cups butternut or acorn squash,
    cooked, cooled, and cubed
1 cup corn
1 cup tomato paste
2 tsp. cumin
2 T. chili powder
1 T. oregano

Place beans in a large Dutch oven. In a frying pan with olive oil, cook the red onion, garlic, and celery until tender. Add to Dutch oven. Add squash, corn, and tomato paste. Stir in enough water to cover. Add seasonings and salt and pepper to taste. Bring to a boil, then cook uncovered for about 2 hours on low heat, stirring occasionally, and adding more water if needed to keep from sticking to bottom. This chili is even better the second day. For an authentic touch, serve with corn bread or corn fritters.

—Nancy V. Bennett

2 Saturday

4th ♋
☽ v/c 11:21 am
☽ enters ♌ 2:21 pm
Color: Blue

Birthday of Timothy Roderick,
Wiccan author

3 Sunday

4th ♌
♃ enters ♍ 2:44 am
☿ enters ♎ 11:04 am
Color: Gold

Dolphins swimming ahead of a ship foretell a safe journey

October

4 Monday

4th ♌
☽ v/c 9:52 am
☽ enters ♍ 4:00 pm
Color: Ivory

President Ronald Reagan signs JR 165 making 1983 "The Year of the Bible" (public law #9728Q); the law states that the Bible is the word of God and urges a return to "traditional" Christian values, 1982

5 Tuesday

4th ♍
Color: Maroon

Rue breaks hexes and grants protection; handle with gloves because the oil can make skin sensitive to sunlight

6 Wednesday

4th ♍
☽ v/c 12:43 pm
☽ enters ♎ 3:52 pm
Color: Yellow

☽ Thursday

4th ♎
♀ enters ♐ 10:11 am
New Moon 2:45 pm
⚶ enters ♏ 9:57 pm
Color: Purple

Birthday of Arnold Crowther, stage magician and Gardnerian Witch, 1909

8 Friday

1st ♎
♀ ℞ 3:05 am
☽ v/c 9:38 am
☽ enters ♏ 3:52 pm
♃ enters ♑ 8:17 pm
Color: Coral

Ivy

The harvest comes to a close during the Celtic month of ivy. Ivy corresponds to the Ogham letter *gort* (gort), bringing the promise of the inner self and the spiral of life. Ivy's growth reflects the spiraling patterns of DNA, the gifts our ancestors gave us. English ivy is evergreen, reminding you that as the world seems to rest, life still remains. Think of your positive attributes, family traits that have served you well. Can you imagine how far the genes you carry have traveled through the ages to form the person that you are? Gaze up at the night sky during this month of ivy—it's the same sky that your most ancient ancestors looked up at. Draw upon the power of Ivy to connect to your ancestors, meditating on their gifts. Listen to any messages they have for you. Repeat the following:

> *I call upon the power of ivy,*
> *The love of my ancestors bind to me,*
> *For part of the past lives on within me,*
> *Spiraling within and around me.*

—Mickie Mueller

---

9 Saturday

1st ♏
Color: Gray

Spilling a box of matches foretells good luck

---

10 Sunday

1st ♏
☽ v/c 2:27 pm
☽ enters ♐ 6:09 pm
Color: Amber

Lotus incense elevates the mood of the mind

October

11 Monday
1st ♐
Color: Lavender

Columbus Day (observed)

12 Tuesday
1st ♐
☽ v/c 8:08 pm
Color: Black

Birthday of Aleister Crowley, 1875

13 Wednesday
1st ♐
☽ enters ♑ 12:17 am
Color: White

Jacques de Molay and other
French Templars arrested by
order of King Phillip IV, 1306

◐ Thursday
1st ♑
2nd quarter 5:27 pm
Color: White

15 Friday
2nd ♑
☽ v/c 5:49 am
☽ enters ♒ 10:24 am
Color: Purple

*Connect with west energy through
dreamwork, sweat lodge ceremonies,
swimming, hypnotism, or visiting sacred springs*

Harvest Pumpkin Pancakes

2 cups self-rising flour
½ cup brown sugar
1 tsp. cinnamon
1 tsp. nutmeg
½ cup canned pumpkin (or ½ cup
    cooked and pureed pumpkin)
2 large farm eggs
1 cup water

Mix the dry ingredients and make a
well in the center. Gradually add your
wet ingredients—the pumpkin and
eggs—ending with water. Mix the water in slowly until you have a nice
thin batter. You may have to add more water if it is too dry.

Preheat a frying pan or griddle to medium heat and coat with a bit of
oil. Drop the pancake batter in by spoonfuls, 2 to 3 per pancake. When
pancake top is bubbly all the way through, it's time to flip it. Cook for a
few seconds until done. You can test this by poking a hole in the middle
and making sure the batter is cooked. Enjoy on a cold autumn morning or
for a seasonal brunch. These are especially nice served with blackberry jam
and a maple butter (soft butter mixed with maple syrup).

—Nancy V. Bennett

---

16 Saturday

2nd ≈
Color: Indigo

*Hops bring healing and sleep; dried hops
make excellent stuffing for dream pillows*

---

17 Sunday

2nd ≈
☽ v/c 2:49 pm
☽ enters ♓ 10:52 pm
Color: Yellow

October

18 Monday
2nd ♓
Color: Silver

Birthday of Nicholas Culpeper,
astrologer and herbalist, 1616

19 Tuesday
2nd ♓
Color: Gray

Water rules the magic of ice,
mirrors, the sea, weather, and oils

20 Wednesday
2nd ♓
☽ v/c 6:25 am
☽ enters ♈ 11:23 am
☿ enters ♏ 5:19 pm
Color: Brown

Birthday of Selena Fox, Circle Sanctuary

21 Thursday
2nd ♈
Color: Crimson

Friday
2nd ♈
☽ v/c 9:37 pm
Full Moon 9:37 pm
☽ enters ♉ 10:30 pm
Color: Pink

Blood Moon

Set in Eastern Daylight Time (EDT)

Blood Moon

To the Cherokee, October is the Harvest Moon, as this is when people gather and preserve most of their food. To the Choctaw, this is the Blackberry Moon. In warmer regions, late-cropping berries ripen now and are often dried or preserved for winter use. The Dakota Sioux call this the Moon When Quilling and Beading Is Done. These creative pursuits take many hours, so people favor them when less outdoor work can be

done but enough daylight still remains to see fine details.

October closes the harvest season as the last grains and other crops come in. Food storage occupies people's attention. Although modern supermarkets are an option, many benefits come from growing and preserving at least some of your own food. Likewise, magical artifacts crafted by the user tend to hold more power than purchased ones. This is also a good time to craft sacred and magical decorations to prepare for winter celebrations.

Rituals often feature the harvest—honoring the fruits of our labors, giving thanks for what we receive, and requesting a bountiful yield. Magically, gather friends for craft workshops to make items for ceremonial use.

—Elizabeth Barrette

---

23 Saturday

3rd ♉
☉ enters ♏ 8:35 am
Color: Brown

Sun enters Scorpio

---

24 Sunday

3rd ♉
Color: Orange

*It is believed that a person born on Samhain
will be able to see and speak with spirits*

October

25 Monday
3rd ♉
☽ v/c 3:49 am
☽ enters ♊ 7:47 am
Color: Ivory

Jacques de Molay first interrogated
after Templar arrest, 1306

26 Tuesday
3rd ♊
Color: Black

De Molay and thirty-one other Templars
confess to heresy in front of an assembly of
clergy; all later recant their confessions, 1306
Sybil Leek, Wiccan author, dies of cancer, 1982

27 Wednesday
3rd ♊
☽ v/c 10:19 am
☽ enters ♋ 3:14 pm
Color: Topaz

Circle Sanctuary founded, 1974

28 Thursday
3rd ♋
♂ enters ♐ 2:48 am
Color: Green

Celtic Tree Month of Reed begins

29 Friday
3rd ♋
☽ v/c 3:48 pm
☽ enters ♌ 8:39 pm
Color: Coral

MacGregor Mathers issues manifesto calling
himself supreme leader of the Golden Dawn; all
members had to sign an oath of fealty to him, 1896
Birthday of Frater Zarathustra,
who founded the Temple of Truth in 1972

114   *Set in Eastern Daylight Time (EDT)*

Samhain

Samhain is the final harvest. It is the Celtic New Year, the time when whatever has not been harvested must be left in the fields for the spirits. It is the night of the Dumb Supper, the Night of the Ancestors, and the night to work with the Dead. It's a night of release, of relief, of grief. It's also a time for fresh starts. You can throw out what hasn't worked, and start anew.

It's the night of Hecate at the crossroads. Are you at a crossroads in your life? Is it time to ask Hecate for guidance? You can do so in ritual or in meditation; but be careful what you ask for. Hecate does not suffer fools gladly. She will give you the answer, whether you're ready for it or not.

Tonight is also a night to reconnect through the generations with your ancestors. Reach back as far as you can and allow them to guide you. The nights immediately after Samhain are good nights to work with the dead, whether they are ancestors or children or pets or lost souls with no one to mourn for them. Cast a circle, light a candle, let them know they are remembered and mourned, and help them complete their journeys. The living can heal the dead by both loving them and letting them go.

—Cerridwen Iris Shea

☽ Saturday

3rd ♌

4th quarter 8:46 am

Color: Gray

House-Senate conferees drop the Senate provision barring the IRS from granting tax-exempt status to groups that promote satanism or witchcraft, 1985

PACT (Pagan Awareness Coalition for Teens) established in Omaha, Nebraska, 2001

---

31 Sunday

4th ♌

☽ v/c 5:01 pm

☽ enters ♍ 11:51 pm

Color: Orange

Samhain/Halloween

Martin Luther nails his ninety-five theses to the door of Wittenburg Castle Church, igniting the Protestant revolution, 1517

Covenant of the Goddess founded, 1975

November

1 Monday
4th ♍
Color: Gray

All Saints' Day
Aquarian Tabernacle Church established in
the United States, 1979

2 Tuesday
4th ♍
☽ v/c 8:36 pm
Color: Red

Election Day (general)
Circle Sanctuary purchases land
for nature preserve, 1983

3 Wednesday
4th ♍
☽ enters ♎ 1:19 am
Color: Yellow

4 Thursday
4th ♎
☽ v/c 7:34 pm
Color: Turquoise

To invoke water, burn Blue Nile incense

5 Friday
4th ♎
☽ enters ♏ 2:16 am
♃ D 2:42 pm
Color: Coral

☽ Saturday

4th ♏

New Moon 12:52 am

☽ v/c 11:44 pm

Color: Blue

7 Sunday

1st ♏

♆ D 1:04 am

☽ enters ♐ 3:28 am

♀ enters ♎ 10:06 pm

Color: Amber

Samhain crossquarter day
(Sun reaches 15° Scorpio)
Daylight Saving Time ends at 2 am

November

8 Monday
1st ♐
☿ enters ♐ 6:43 pm
Color: Silver

Sentencing of Witches in
Basque Zugarramurdi trial, 1610

Marriage of Patricia and Arnold Crowther
officiated by Gerald Gardner, 1960

9 Tuesday
1st ♐
☽ v/c 7:35 am
☽ enters ♑ 8:37 am
Color: Maroon

Patricia and Arnold Crowther
married in civil ceremony, 1960

10 Wednesday
1st ♑
Color: Topaz

11 Thursday
1st ♑
☽ v/c 2:57 pm
☽ enters ♒ 5:32 pm
Color: Green

Veterans Day

12 Friday
1st ♒
Color: Purple

Use violet to promote self-awareness,
spiritual growth, and deep healing

Reed

The cold snap in the air marks the Celtic month of reed. Reed corresponds to the Ogham letter *ngtal* (nyeh-dl) and is also associated with the broom. Reed was used to thatch the roofs of homes and to sometimes sweep floors in ancient times; reed can symbolize action taken as well as hearth and home. We tend to get overwhelmed during the busy holiday season, so this is a good time to work with this month's energies.

First, sweep all around your home, brushing away all negativity out the back door. Then tie a few stems of dried reed to a decorative broom (all obtained at your local craft store) and hang it in your kitchen to fend off family stress and anxiety over the holidays, visualize it filling the house with harmonious energy. To charge it, repeat:

> *Reed and broom direct us away from trouble,*
> *Fill this home with harmony on the double.*
> *Protect and bless us day and nightly,*
> *Facing the oncoming winter brightly.*

—Mickie Mueller

☾ Saturday

1st ≈
2nd quarter 11:39 am
Color: Gray

When working water magic, use dilution,
aspersion, washing, or magical baths

---

14 Sunday

2nd ≈
☽ v/c 1:33 am
☽ enters ♓ 5:24 am
Color: Yellow

November

15 Monday

2nd ♓
Color: Lavender

Aquarian Tabernacle Church
established in Canada, 1993

16 Tuesday

2nd ♓
☽ v/c 11:37 am
☽ enters ♈ 5:59 pm
Color: Black

Night of Hecate

17 Wednesday
2nd ♈
Color: White

Birthday of Israel Regardie, occultist
and member of the OTO, 1907

18 Thursday
2nd ♈
♃ D 11:53 am
♀ D 4:18 pm
Color: Purple

Aleister Crowley initiated into the
Golden Dawn as Frater Perdurabo, 1898

19 Friday

2nd ♈
☽ v/c 12:33 am
☽ enters ♉ 5:04 am
Color: Rose

Birthday of Theodore
Parker Mills, Wiccan elder, 1924

Set in Eastern Standard Time (EST)

Mourning Moon

In Cherokee tradition, November is the Trading Moon. With the harvest in and necessary foods stocked up, this time before the full force of winter arrives is ideal for visiting and exchanging goods. To the Choctaw, this is the Sassafras Moon. When the mitten-shaped leaves turn orange and drop off, that's a good time to harvest the roots for flavoring beverages. The Dakota Sioux call this the Moon When Horns Are Broken Off. This may refer to the broken antlers that occur when bucks fight over mates.

During November, the earth goes dormant. Many plants die back. People and animals begin relying more on stored foods and fat reserves. Several species of large animals have their mating season in late autumn or early winter. Offer suet and other high-nutrient foods to wildlife.

Magically, work spells relating to animals active at this time, such as deer totems. A piece of deerskin leather or some antler buttons can enhance the connection. Hunting charms are appropriate for people who still hunt some of their own food. Rituals may celebrate animals spirits or the introspective energy of the dormant season.

—Elizabeth Barrette

---

20 Saturday

2nd ♉
Color: Brown

Church of All Worlds
incorporates in Australia, 1992

☺ Sunday

2nd ♉
☽ v/c 12:27 pm
Full Moon 12:27 pm
☽ enters ♊ 1:46 pm
Color: Gold

Mourning Moon

---

22 Monday

3rd ♊
☉ enters ♐ 5:15 am
Color: White

Sun enters Sagittarius

The first pentacle in a VA cemetery is
granted to Patrick Stewart in Nevada; the
governor approved the plaque in the state
cemetery prior to nationwide approval, 2006

23 Tuesday

3rd ♊
☽ v/c 4:56 pm
☽ enters ♋ 8:14 pm
Color: Gray

Birthday of Lady Tamara Von Forslun,
founder of the Church of Wicca and the
Aquarian Tabernacle Church in Australia

24 Wednesday

3rd ♋
Color: Brown

25 Thursday

3rd ♋
☽ v/c 10:44 pm
Color: Crimson

Thanksgiving Day
Celtic Tree Month of Elder begins
Dr. John Dee notes Edward
Kelley's death in his diary, 1595

26 Friday

3rd ♋
☽ enters ♌ 1:01 am
Color: Pink

27 Saturday

3rd ♌
Color: Gray

☽ Sunday

3rd ♌
☽ v/c 3:30 am
☽ enters ♍ 4:34 am
4th quarter 3:36 pm
Color: Amber

Almonds convey wisdom;
candied almonds are traditional holiday treats

29 Monday
4th ♍
♀ enters ♏ 7:33 pm
Color: Ivory

30 Tuesday
4th ♍
☽ v/c 6:17 am
☽ enters ♎ 7:15 am
☿ enters ♑ 7:10 pm
Color: Black

Birthday of Oberon Zell,
Church of All Worlds

Father Urbain Grandier imprisoned in
France for bewitching nuns, 1633

1 Wednesday
4th ♎
Color: Yellow

Birthday of Anodea Judith,
president, Church of All Worlds

2 Thursday
4th ♎
☽ v/c 3:08 am
☽ enters ♏ 9:44 am
Color: Green

Hanukkah begins

3 Friday
4th ♏
♆ enters ♐ 2:29 am
Color: White

Elder

The close of the year is nigh; we end with the Celtic month of elder. Elder corresponds to the Ogham letter *ruis* (roo-ish), which allows us to examine all the things we may regret, properly view the consequences, and heal our heart from the hurt. Elder ushers in a new phase of life and reminds us of the need to let go of what no longer serves you. To release past errors and go forward with joy in your heart, light a red candle, and surround it with

elderberries or a picture of an elder tree. You may wish to sip some elderberry wine or tea. Write down the things that didn't go as planned this year and what you learned from each one. Draw the elder/ruis Ogham symbol on top of the paper. Bury the paper in the earth—as the paper becomes one with the earth, your regrets will dissipate and your heart will heal.

> *Elder tree, berries of red,*
> *Remove these worries from my head.*
> *Wiser now I do remain,*
> *I banish regret and send it away!*

—Mickie Mueller

---

4 Saturday

4th ♏
☽ v/c 7:13 am
☽ enters ♐ 12:59 pm
Color: Gray

☽ Sunday

4th ♐
New Moon 12:36 pm
♅ D 8:50 pm
Color: Yellow

Pope Innocent VIII reverses the
Canon Episcopi by issuing the bull
Summis Desiderantes Affectibus, removing
obstacles to Inquisitors, 1484
Death of Aleister Crowley, 1947

December

6 Monday

1st ♐
☽ v/c 4:46 pm
☽ enters ♑ 6:16 pm
Color: White

Death of Jacob Sprenger, coauthor
of the *Malleus Maleficarum*, 1495

Birthday of Dion Fortune, member
of the Golden Dawn, 1890

7 Tuesday

1st ♑
♂ enters ♑ 6:49 pm
Color: Gray

Islamic New Year

8 Wednesday

1st ♑
☽ v/c 8:07 pm
Color: Brown

9 Thursday

1st ♑
☽ enters ♒ 2:30 am
Color: Crimson

Hanukkah ends

10 Friday

1st ♒
☿ ℞ 7:04 am
Color: White

Ye Gods! Cranberry Ambrosia

Even a winter god or goddess needs a little taste of immortality, too! Here is a recipe using seasonal fruit (cranberry and mandarin oranges) to end your yuletide feast on a festive note.

8 oz. can pineapple tidbits, drained
2 mandarin oranges, segmented
½ cup maraschino cherries, chopped
1 can cranberry sauce with berries, chopped
8 oz. sour cream
1½ cups fresh whipped cream
2 T. lemon juice
½ cup whipped cream
½ cup fresh cranberries
½ cup toasted coconut

Combine pineapple, oranges, cherries, and cranberry sauce. Mix in the sour cream, whipped cream, and lemon juice and chill in the refrigerator for at least 2 hours. Before serving, smooth the additional whipped cream on top and garnish with fresh cranberries and coconut. Serves 4.

—Nancy V. Bennett

11 Saturday
1st ≈
☽ v/c 6:09 am
☽ enters ♓ 1:41 pm
Color: Indigo

Caves, forests, farms, nurseries, basements,
and kitchens enhance earth energy

12 Sunday
1st ♓
Color: Orange

December

◐ Monday
1st ♓
2nd quarter 8:59 am
☽ v/c 7:35 pm
Color: Gray

First papal bull against black magic
issued by Alexander IV, 1258

14 Tuesday
2nd ♓
☽ enters ♈ 2:15 am
Color: Black

15 Wednesday
2nd ♈
Color: Topaz

16 Thursday
2nd ♈
☽ v/c 6:41 am
☽ enters ♉ 1:49 pm
Color: Purple

A Yule log must be found, not
purchased, and once lit must continue
burning until completely consumed

17 Friday
2nd ♉
Color: Pink

Yule

We deck our halls and our porches and our garage roofs with lights to ward off the dark. We celebrate the rebirth of the light on this longest night. The Winter Solstice, a time for gathering, love, peace, goodwill, and most importantly, forgiveness, is now. During this cold and barren time, we bring in greenery to symbolize life. We use bright colors, depictions of a bountiful harvest, and piles of presents to stave off want or the fear of want.

This Yuletide season, go back through photo albums, yearbooks, and address books. Find people with whom you've lost touch. Take ten minutes and write a card with a short, personal greeting to reconnect.

On the Solstice itself, light as many candles as you can safely in your space. At some point in your ceremony, extinguish all of them. Sit in the dark for a few moments, contemplating darkness, the dark night of the soul, and what it means to you. Relight the candles, beginning with one central to the rite, then move around your space clockwise, lighting them to symbolize the turn of the wheel back toward daylight. Perform divination with the candles out, and let relighting the candles symbolize your own enlightenment.

—Cerridwen Iris Shea

---

18 Saturday

2nd ☿
☿ enters ♐ 9:53 am
☽ v/c 4:37 pm
☽ enters ♊ 10:37 pm
Color: Blue

Bananas increase both fertility and potency

---

19 Sunday

2nd ♊
Color: Gold

Lavender oil helps neutralize unwanted sexual energies

December

20 Monday
2nd ♊
♀ enters ♑ 5:28 pm
Color: Lavender

Decorate with orange to boost energy and zest for life

☻ Tuesday
2nd ♊
☽ v/c 3:13 am
Full Moon 3:13 am
☽ enters ♋ 4:22 am
☉ enters ♑ 6:38 pm
Color: White

Yule/Winter Solstice
Long Nights Moon
Sun enters Capricorn
Lunar eclipse 3:17 am, 29° ♊ 22'
Janet and Stewart Farrar begin their first coven together, 1970

22 Wednesday
3rd ♋
Color: Brown

Celtic Tree Month of Elder ends

23 Thursday
3rd ♋
☽ v/c 2:25 am
☽ enters ♌ 7:51 am
Color: Turquoise

Between (Celtic Tree Month)

24 Friday
3rd ♌
Color: Rose

Christmas Eve
Celtic Tree Month of Birch begins

Set in Eastern Standard Time (EST)

Long Nights Moon

To the Cherokee, December is the Snow Moon. In southern regions, the rare snowfall most often occurs during this time of year. The Choctaw refer to this as the Peach Moon. To the Dakota Sioux, it is simply the Twelfth Moon.

December marks the onset of winter. The world turns dark and cold. Plants have gone dormant; trees stand bare of leaves. Many animals hibernate; others have migrated to distant regions. Game is difficult to find, and hunters may spend long cold hours in the woods with no reward. Fresh food becomes difficult to find in the wild. Yet winter has its own austere beauty in the cool blue shadows and pristine snowdrifts, the glint of icicles, and the delicate feathers of frost.

Rituals in December take an introspective turn. Meditate on what you have done the previous year. Honor death and dormancy as natural parts of the cycle along with life and growth. Admire the splendor of sunlight on the snow and ice. Magically, work spells to "freeze" bad habits and make them go dormant. If you're hanging birdfeeders and putting out water, add a charm to show the birds where these resources are.

—Elizabeth Barrette

---

25 Saturday

3rd ♌
☽ v/c 4:28 am
☽ enters ♍ 10:14 am
Color: Black

Christmas Day
Feast of Frau Holle, Germanic weather goddess
who was believed to travel through
the world to watch people's deeds;
she blessed the good and punished the bad

---

26 Sunday

3rd ♍
Color: Orange

Kwanzaa begins
Dr. Fian arraigned for twenty counts
of witchcraft and treason, 1590

○ Monday
3rd ♍
☽ v/c 7:21 am
☽ enters ♎ 12:38 pm
4th quarter 11:18 pm
Color: Silver

Birthday of Gerina Dunwich,
Wiccan author

28 Tuesday
4th ♎
Color: Scarlet

*Dance around a tree on New Year's
Day to bring love, prosperity, and
health for the next twelve months*

29 Wednesday
4th ♎
☽ v/c 10:05 am
☽ enters ♏ 3:49 pm
Color: Yellow

30 Thursday
4th ♏
☿ D 2:21 am
Color: White

31 Friday
4th ♏
☽ v/c 2:57 pm
☽ enters ♐ 8:21 pm
Color: Purple

New Year's Eve

1 Saturday

4th ♐

Color: Gray

New Year's Day

Kwanzaa ends

2 Sunday

4th ♐

☽ v/c 9:08 pm

Color: Gold

About the Authors

ELIZABETH BARRETTE, the managing editor of *PanGaia*, has been involved with the Pagan community for twenty years, actively networking via coffeehouse meetings and open sabbats. Her other writing includes speculative fiction and gender studies. Her 2005 poem "The Poltergeist of Polaris" earned a nomination for the Rhysling Award. She lives in central Illinois and enjoys herbal landscaping and gardening for wildlife.

NANCY V. BENNETT is a longtime Llewellyn annuals writer whose work has also appeared in *We'moon*, Circle network, and many mainstream publications. Her pet projects include reading and writing about history and creating ethnic dinners to test on her family. She lives near a protected salmon stream where the deer and bears often play.

TABITHA BRADLEY is an Arizona author who has been writing science fiction and Pagan nonfiction for more than ten years. Her work has appeared in *Llewellyn's Witches' Calendar* and she is the author of the popular, award-winning *Dirandan Chronicles* series from Renaissance E-Books. She is also a professional tarot reader, Pagan teacher, and practicing Witch. She has been a guest at Arizona-based science-fiction conventions, where she has spoken on Pagan as well as science fiction and fantasy topics. Visit Tabitha's art gallery, book and article listings at her Web site, Diranda Studios at www.diranda.com.

ELLEN DUGAN, the "Garden Witch," is a psychic-clairvoyant and a practicing Witch of twenty years. Ellen is a master gardener who teaches flower folklore and gardening at a community college and is the author of several Llewellyn books, including: *Garden Witchery, Elements of Witchcraft, 7 Days of Magic, The Enchanted Cat, Herb Magic for Beginners,* and *Natural Witchery.* Ellen and her family live in Missouri.

MAGENTA GRIFFITH has been a Witch for nearly thirty years and is a founding member of the coven Prodea, which has celebrated rituals since 1980. She has been a member of the Covenant of the Goddess, the Covenant of Unitarian Universalist Pagans, and Church of All Worlds. She presents workshops and classes at festivals around the Midwest.

JENNIFER HEWITSON has been a freelance illustrator since 1985. Her illustrations have appeared in local and national publications, including the *Wall Street Journal,* the *Washington Post,* the *Los Angeles Times, US News & World Report,* and *Ladybug* magazine. Her advertising and packaging clients include Disney and the San Diego Zoo. Jennifer has created a line of greeting cards for Sun Rise Publications, and has illustrated several children's books. Her work has been recognized by numerous organizations, including the Society of Illustrators Los Angeles, and magazines such as *Communication Arts, Print,* and *How.*

JAMES KAMBOS is a writer and folk artist based in Ohio. He is a longtime contributor to Llewellyn's annuals, and enjoys writing about magic, herbs, and folklore traditions. When not writing and painting, James enjoys cooking using the vegetables and herbs he raises himself.

MICKIE MUELLER is an award-winning Pagan spiritual artist. She is a High Priestess, an ordained Pagan Minister and a Reiki master/teacher. She is the illustrator of the critically acclaimed divination decks, *The Well Worn Path* and *The Hidden Path.* She is also the writer and illustrator of the upcoming *The Voice of the Trees: A Celtic Ogham Oracle.* Her magical artwork can be seen on her Web site at www.mickiemuellerart.com.

DIANA RAJCHEL lives, works, worships, and writes in Minneapolis, Minnesota. She is the organizer of the Twin Cities Urban Magic Project and also assists in the planning of Twin Cities Pagan Pride. Sometimes she works with organizations that need assistance in the care and feeding of volunteers. You can learn more about her at www.dianarajchel.com.

CERRIDWEN IRIS SHEA writes, teaches tarot, cooks, and enjoys ice hockey and thoroughbred racing. Besides writing for Llewellyn annuals since 1994, her work has also been published in *Emerging Women Writers, The Scruffy Dog Review, Of Like Mind,* and *Circle.* For more, visit her tarot blog, *Kemmyrk* http://kemmyrk.wordpress.com and her Web site, *Cerridwen's Cottage,* www.cerridwenscottage.com.

Appendix

Daily Magical Influences

Each day is ruled by a planet with specific magical influences.
Monday (Moon): peace, healing, caring, psychic awareness
Tuesday (Mars): passion, courage, aggression, protection
Wednesday (Mercury): study, travel, divination, wisdom
Thursday (Jupiter): expansion, money, prosperity, generosity
Friday (Venus): love, friendship, reconciliation, beauty
Saturday (Saturn): longevity, endings, homes
Sunday (Sun): healing, spirituality, success, strength, protection

Color Correspondences

Colors are associated with each day, according to planetary influence.
Monday: gray, lavender, white, silver, ivory
Tuesday: red, white, black, gray, maroon, scarlet
Wednesday: yellow, brown, white, topaz
Thursday: green, turquoise, white, purple, crimson
Friday: white, pink, rose, purple, coral
Saturday: brown, gray, blue, indigo, black
Sunday: yellow, orange, gold, amber

Lunar Phases

Waxing, from New Moon to Full Moon, is the ideal time to do magic to draw things to you.

Waning, from Full Moon to New Moon, is a time for study, meditation, and magical work designed to banish harmful energies.

The Moon's Sign

The Moon continuously moves through each sign of the zodiac, from Aries to Pisces, staying about two and a half days in each sign. The Moon influences the sign it inhabits, creating different energies that affect our day-to-day lives.

Aries: Good for starting things. Things occur rapidly, but quickly pass. People tend to be argumentative and assertive.

Taurus: Things begun now last longest, tend to increase in value, and become hard to change. Brings out an appreciation for beauty and sensory experience.

Gemini: Things begun now are easily changed by outside influence. Time for shortcuts, communication, games, and fun.

Cancer: Stimulates emotional rapport between people. Supports growth and nurturing. Tend to domestic concerns.

Leo: Draws emphasis to the self, to central ideas or institutions, away from connections with others and emotional needs.

Virgo: Favors accomplishment of details and commands from higher up. Focus on health, hygiene, and daily schedules.

Libra: Favors cooperation, compromise, social activities, balance, friendship, and partnership.

Scorpio: Increases awareness of psychic power. Precipitates psychic crises and ends connections thoroughly. People have a tendency to brood and become secretive.

Sagittarius: Encourages confidence and flights of imagination. This is an adventurous, philosophical, and athletic Moon sign. Favors expansion and growth.

Capricorn: Develops strong structure. Focus on traditions, responsibilities, and obligations. A good time to set boundaries and rules.

Aquarius: Rebellious energy. Time to break habits and make abrupt change. Personal freedom and individuality is the focus.

Pisces: The focus is on dreaming, nostalgia, intuition, and psychic impressions. A good time for spiritual or philanthropic activities.

2010 Eclipses

January 15, 2:07 am; Solar eclipse 25° ♑ 02'
June 26, 7:38 am; Lunar eclipse 4° ♑ 50'
July 11, 3:33 pm; Solar eclipse 19° ♋ 24'
December 21, 3:17 am; Lunar eclipse 29° ♊ 22'

2010 Full Moons

Cold Moon: January 30, 1:18 am
Quickening Moon: February 28, 11:38 am
Storm Moon: March 29, 10:25 pm
Wind Moon: April 28, 8:19 am
Flower Moon: May 27, 7:07 pm
Strong Sun Moon: June 26, 7:30 am
Blessing Moon: July 25, 9:37 pm
Corn Moon: August 24, 1:05 pm
Harvest Moon: September 23, 5:17 am
Blood Moon: October 22, 9:37 pm
Mourning Moon: November 21, 12:27 pm
Long Nights Moon: December 21, 3:13 am

Planetary Retrogrades in 2010

Mars	℞	12/20/09	8:26 am	—	Direct	03/10/10	12:09 pm
Mercury	℞	12/26/09	9:38 am	—	Direct	01/15/10	11:52 am
Saturn	℞	01/13/10	10:56 am	—	Direct	05/30/10	2:09 pm
Pluto	℞	04/06/10	10:34 pm	—	Direct	09/14/10	12:37 am
Mercury	℞	04/18/10	12:06 am	—	Direct	05/11/10	6:27 pm
Neptune	℞	05/31/10	2:48 pm	—	Direct	11/07/10	1:04 am
Uranus	℞	07/05/10	12:50 pm	—	Direct	12/05/10	8:50 pm
Jupiter	℞	07/23/10	8:03 am	—	Direct	11/18/10	11:53 am
Mercury	℞	08/20/10	3:59 pm	—	Direct	09/12/10	7:09 pm
Venus	℞	10/08/10	3:05 pm	—	Direct	11/18/10	4:18 pm
Mercury	℞	12/10/10	7:04 am	—	Direct	12/30/10	2:21 am

Moon Void-of-Course Data for 2010

JANUARY

Last Aspect Date	Time	New Sign	New Time
1	10:43 am	1 ♌	9:41 pm
3	4:55 pm	3 ♍	9:52 pm
5	12:25 pm	5 ♎	11:58 pm
8	1:07 am	8 ♏	5:00 am
10	10:02 am	10 ♐	1:10 pm
12	9:43 pm	12 ♑	11:54 pm
15	4:02 am	15 ♒	12:17 pm
17	3:22 pm	18 ♓	1:17 am
20	1:06 am	20 ♈	1:36 pm
22	2:46 pm	22 ♉	11:39 pm
24	10:03 pm	25 ♊	6:11 am
27	1:32 am	27 ♋	9:01 am
28	11:49 pm	29 ♌	9:10 am
31	1:27 am	31 ♍	8:23 am

FEBRUARY

Last Aspect Date	Time	New Sign	New Time
1	11:17 pm	2 ♎	8:42 am
4	4:27 am	4 ♏	11:56 am
6	11:11 am	6 ♐	7:04 pm
8	11:58 pm	9 ♑	5:43 am
11	7:39 am	11 ♒	6:24 pm
13	11:33 pm	14 ♓	7:23 am
16	9:32 am	16 ♈	7:30 pm
18	10:52 pm	19 ♉	5:55 am
21	7:15 am	21 ♊	1:47 pm
23	12:29 pm	23 ♋	6:29 pm
25	12:48 pm	25 ♌	8:08 pm
27	3:15 pm	27 ♍	7:52 pm

MARCH

Last Aspect Date	Time	New Sign	New Time
1	12:36 pm	1 ♎	7:31 pm
3	3:43 pm	3 ♏	9:11 pm
5	11:32 pm	6 ♐	2:29 am
8	6:13 am	8 ♑	12:13 pm
10	4:59 pm	11 ♒	12:42 am
13	7:57 am	13 ♓	1:44 pm
15	8:01 pm	16 ♈	2:32 am
18	7:23 am	18 ♉	12:29 pm
20	3:41 pm	20 ♊	8:28 pm
22	9:49 pm	23 ♋	2:16 am
25	12:39 am	25 ♌	5:39 am
27	3:04 am	27 ♍	6:57 am
29	2:55 am	29 ♎	7:21 am
31	8:13 am	31 ♏	8:41 am

APRIL

Last Aspect Date	Time	New Sign	New Time
2	8:54 am	2 ♐	12:53 pm
4	4:57 pm	4 ♑	9:07 pm
7	4:18 am	7 ♒	8:51 am
9	5:44 pm	9 ♓	9:48 pm
12	8:51 am	12 ♈	9:31 am
14	3:23 pm	14 ♉	6:55 pm
17	12:57 am	17 ♊	2:08 am
19	1:24 am	19 ♋	7:39 am
21	10:07 am	21 ♌	11:42 am
23	11:35 am	23 ♍	2:24 pm
25	2:21 pm	25 ♎	4:16 pm
27	3:45 pm	27 ♏	6:28 pm
29	8:39 pm	29 ♐	10:36 pm

MAY

Last Aspect Date	Time	New Sign	New Time
2	4:08 am	2 ♑	6:00 am
4	3:07 pm	4 ♒	4:52 pm
7	2:36 am	7 ♓	5:34 am
9	4:12 pm	9 ♈	5:29 pm
12	12:11 am	12 ♉	2:48 am
14	8:28 am	14 ♊	9:18 am
16	1:06 pm	16 ♋	1:46 pm
18	4:35 pm	18 ♌	5:06 pm
20	7:43 pm	20 ♍	7:58 pm
22	10:34 pm	22 ♎	10:50 pm
25	12:01 am	25 ♏	2:17 am
27	7:13 am	27 ♐	7:15 am
29	12:40 pm	29 ♑	2:44 pm
31	11:41 pm	6/1 ♒	1:08 am

JUNE

Last Aspect Date	Time	New Sign	New Time
5/31	11:41 am	1 ♒	1:08 am
3	10:56 am	3 ♓	1:34 pm
6	1:49 am	6 ♈	1:50 am
8	9:13 am	8 ♉	11:41 am
10	3:50 pm	10 ♊	6:11 pm
12	7:35 pm	12 ♋	9:50 pm
14	8:38 pm	14 ♌	11:54 pm
16	11:24 pm	17 ♍	1:41 am
19	1:04 am	19 ♎	4:13 am
21	5:44 am	21 ♏	8:14 am
23	11:32 am	23 ♐	2:10 pm
25	7:33 pm	25 ♑	10:21 pm
28	5:56 am	28 ♒	8:52 am
30	6:03 pm	30 ♓	9:10 am

JULY

Last Aspect Date	Time	New Sign	New Time
3	7:17 am	3 ♈	9:44 am
5	5:24 pm	5 ♉	8:29 pm
8	2:10 am	8 ♊	3:51 am
10	6:17 am	10 ♋	7:38 am
12	7:48 am	12 ♌	8:53 am
14	6:23 am	14 ♍	9:15 am
16	9:46 am	16 ♎	10:24 am
18	10:26 am	18 ♏	1:42 pm
20	7:43 pm	20 ♐	7:58 pm
23	12:50 am	23 ♑	4:39 am
25	10:20 am	25 ♒	3:38 pm
27	11:46 pm	28 ♓	4:00 am
29	11:44 pm	30 ♈	4:42 pm

AUGUST

Last Aspect Date	Time	New Sign	New Time
1	11:54 pm	2 ♉	4:13 am
4	8:44 am	4 ♊	12:54 pm
6	5:22 pm	6 ♋	5:50 pm
7	2:46 pm	8 ♌	7:23 pm
10	3:10 pm	10 ♍	7:01 pm
11	8:04 pm	12 ♎	6:43 pm
14	4:06 pm	14 ♏	8:26 pm
17	1:24 am	17 ♐	1:44 am
19	9:58 am	19 ♑	10:17 am
21	9:08 pm	21 ♒	9:37 pm
24	4:29 am	24 ♓	10:11 am
26	10:00 pm	26 ♈	10:49 pm
29	4:47 am	29 ♉	10:35 am
31	7:13 pm	31 ♊	8:19 pm

SEPTEMBER

Last Aspect Date	Time	New Sign	New Time
3	1:40 am	3 ♋	2:50 am
5	4:31 am	5 ♌	5:45 am
7	4:17 am	7 ♍	5:53 am
9	4:59 am	9 ♎	5:01 am
11	1:16 am	11 ♏	5:21 am
13	7:53 am	13 ♐	8:52 am
15	2:52 pm	15 ♑	4:30 pm
18	1:13 am	18 ♒	3:35 am
20	9:09 am	20 ♓	4:15 pm
23	1:52 am	23 ♈	4:47 am
25	9:12 am	25 ♉	4:17 pm
27	11:03 pm	28 ♊	2:10 am
30	6:37 am	30 ♋	9:46 am

OCTOBER

Last Aspect Date	Time	New Sign	New Time
2	11:21 am	2 ♌	2:21 pm
4	9:52 am	4 ♍	4:00 pm
6	12:43 pm	6 ♎	3:52 pm
8	9:38 am	8 ♏	3:52 pm
10	2:27 pm	10 ♐	6:09 pm
12	8:08 pm	13 ♑	12:17 am
15	5:49 am	15 ♒	10:24 am
17	2:49 pm	17 ♓	10:52 pm
20	6:25 am	20 ♈	11:23 am
22	9:37 pm	22 ♉	10:30 pm
25	3:49 am	25 ♊	7:47 am
27	10:19 am	27 ♋	3:14 pm
29	3:48 pm	29 ♌	8:39 pm
31	5:01 pm	31 ♍	11:51 pm

NOVEMBER

Last Aspect Date	Time	New Sign	New Time
2	8:36 pm	3 ♎	1:19 am
4	7:34 pm	5 ♏	2:16 am
6	11:44 pm	7 ♐	3:28 am
9	7:35 am	9 ♑	8:37 am
11	2:57 pm	11 ♒	5:32 pm
13	11:33 am	14 ♓	5:24 am
16	11:37 am	16 ♈	5:59 pm
19	12:33 am	19 ♉	5:04 am
21	12:27 pm	21 ♊	1:46 pm
23	4:56 pm	23 ♋	8:14 pm
25	10:44 pm	26 ♌	1:01 am
28	3:30 am	28 ♍	4:34 am
30	6:17 am	30 ♎	7:15 am

DECEMBER

Last Aspect Date	Time	New Sign	New Time
2	3:08 am	2 ♏	9:44 am
4	7:13 am	4 ♐	12:59 pm
6	4:46 pm	6 ♑	6:16 pm
8	8:07 pm	9 ♒	2:30 am
11	6:09 am	11 ♓	1:41 pm
13	7:35 pm	14 ♈	2:15 am
16	6:41 am	16 ♉	1:49 pm
18	4:37 pm	18 ♊	10:37 pm
21	3:13 am	21 ♋	4:22 am
23	2:25 am	23 ♌	7:51 am
25	4:28 am	25 ♍	10:14 am
27	7:21 am	27 ♎	12:38 pm
29	10:05 am	29 ♏	3:49 pm
31	2:57 pm	31 ♐	8:21 pm

Set in Eastern Time. All times corrected for Daylight Saving Time.

365 Spells, Meditations, Recipes, Holidays, and Lore

Give every day a magical lift with a spell from *Llewellyn's 2010 Witches' Spell-A-Day Almanac*. Elizabeth Barrette, Ellen Dugan, Raven Digitalis and other Wiccan experts offer spells for every occasion—all easy to use with minimal supplies. Each spell is categorized by purpose: health, love, money, protection, and more. You'll also find recipes, rituals, and meditations to fortify your daily practice. Astrological data is included for those who wish to boost their magic with planetary energy.

Name:

Address, City, State, Zip:

Home Phone: Office Phone:

E-mail: Birthday:

Name:

Address, City, State, Zip:

Home Phone: Office Phone:

E-mail: Birthday:

Name:

Address, City, State, Zip:

Home Phone: Office Phone:

E-mail: Birthday:

Name:

Address, City, State, Zip:

Home Phone: Office Phone:

E-mail: Birthday:

Name:

Address, City, State, Zip:

Home Phone: Office Phone:

E-mail: Birthday:

Name:

Address, City, State, Zip:

Home Phone: Office Phone:

E-mail: Birthday:

Name:

Address, City, State, Zip:

Home Phone: Office Phone:

E-mail: Birthday:

Name:

Address, City, State, Zip:

Home Phone: Office Phone:

E-mail: Birthday:

Name:

Address, City, State, Zip:

Home Phone: Office Phone:

E-mail: Birthday:

Name:

Address, City, State, Zip:

Home Phone: Office Phone:

E-mail: Birthday:

Name:

Address, City, State, Zip:

Home Phone: Office Phone:

E-mail: Birthday:

Name:

Address, City, State, Zip:

Home Phone: Office Phone:

E-mail: Birthday:

Name:

Address, City, State, Zip:

Home Phone: Office Phone:

E-mail: Birthday:

Name:

Address, City, State, Zip:

Home Phone: Office Phone:

E-mail: Birthday:

Name:

Address, City, State, Zip:

Home Phone: Office Phone:

E-mail: Birthday:

Name:

Address, City, State, Zip:

Home Phone: Office Phone:

E-mail: Birthday:

Name:

Address, City, State, Zip:

Home Phone: Office Phone:

E-mail: Birthday:

Name:

Address, City, State, Zip:

Home Phone: Office Phone:

E-mail: Birthday: